Spellbound

Spellbound
The Art of
Teaching Poetry

Edited by
Matthew Burgess

"A handbook for sneaking up on the mysteries."
— Edward Hirsch

TEACHERS
&WRITERS
COLLABORATIVE

T&W Books
New York

For the teachers who bring poetry into the room,
and for the students who respond in kind.

Spellbound: The Art of Teaching Poetry

The permissions acknowledgments on pages 234–237 constitute an extension of the copyright page.

Library of Congress Cataloguing-in-Publication Data

Burgess, Matthew (1973–
Spellbound: the art of teaching poetry / Matthew Burgess
     ISBN-13: 978-0-915924-83-7 (ppk-alk.paper)
     ISBN-10: 0-915924-83-8 (ppk-alk.paper)
                    2018967095

Teachers & Writers Collaborative
540 President Street, 3rd Floor
Brooklyn, NY 11215

Cover image: Ping Zhu
Design: L+L (landl.us)

Printed by Lightning Source

Acknowledgments

Spellbound exists because of the creativity and expertise of the writer-teachers who have contributed to this collection. First and foremost, we wish to thank you for taking the time to share your methods with such thoughtful detail. Our sincere gratitude to the student poets whose work is included as well; your poems are sure to inspire many others. Special shout-out to T&W's executive director, Amy Swauger, for collaborating and assisting with the making of this book at every step. Thank you to T&W staff Jade Triton and Jordan Dann; to the T&W editorial associates Cynthia Amoah, Evan Dent, Victoria Richards, and Ethan Victor; to our designers, Leigh Mignogna, Liz Seibert Turow, and Drew Litowitz; and to Ping Zhu for the cover Illustration. The editor also wishes to thank Ron Padgett, Reza Memari, Jeffrey Rosales, Melanie Maria Goodreaux, James Lecesne, Ellen Tremper, Elaine Brooks, Roni Natov, Dorothea Lasky, Timothy Donnelly, and Mollee Merrill.

Thank you to for The Cerimon Fund for supporting our vision and making this book possible.

Table of Contents

xiii   **Introduction**

xvii   **How to Use This Book**

01   **What Is a Poem?** Writing Towards a Wilder Definition of Poetry
        Erika Luckert

11   **Finding Your Voices** How Jericho Brown, Diana Ross, and Janis Joplin
        Can Inspire Student Writing
        Tiphanie Yanique

18   **The Lune Link** Illuminating Classroom Content with Flashes of Poetry
        Susan Karwoska

29   **Ode to This Body Singing** Teaching Yusef Komunyakaa's "Anodyne"
        Aracelis Girmay

35   **Poetic Introductions** Three Self-Portrait Prompts to Break the Ice
        Emily Moore

45   **"Love Is a Big Blue Cadillac"** Using Metaphor to Explore Concrete
        and Abstract Nouns
        Peter Markus

57   **Inspired by Inkblots** Interpreting Visual Images as a Springboard
        to Poetry
        Chris Cander

64   **A Dramatic reVISION** Reviving Revision through Storytelling
        and Poetry
        Caron Levis

74   **You Are Not You** A Workshop on Ekphrastic Persona and Repetition
        Joanna Fuhrman

82 **"Hanging Fire"** Using Repetition to Write Poems about the Past
Jasminne Mendez

89 **Your Secret Hideout** Poems about Real and Imaginary Childhood Spaces
Matthew Burgess

99 **If I Was a Bird** A Lesson in Self-Definition
Amina Henry

106 **Blues Poems** Borrowing from Song to Write about What's Wrong
Sheila Maldonado

117 **"The Truth" and "first time"** Two Prompts That Invite Emotion and Reflection
Sarah Dohrmann

126 **The One-Sentence Poem** Capturing the Motion of the Mind
Jason Koo

136 **"i know i am in love again when"** Sparking Strange Play through Multi-Media Poetry
Cait Weiss Orcutt

142 **The Poetics of Liberation** Looking Back to Envision the Future
Alex Cuff

151 **History and All Its Bright Particulars** Letter Writing and Poetry
Tina Cane

161 **Wish You Were Here!** Using Postcards to Inspire Poetry
Bianca Stone

168 **Beatbox and Other Experiments** A List of Poetry Prompts
Todd Colby

172 **Wild Thing** Love Poems and Self-Portraits Inspired
by Donika Kelly's *Bestiary*
Melissa Febos

178 **Lost and Found** Reading and Writing the Elegy
Michael Morse

191 **Imaginary Gallery** A Collaborative Writing Exercise
Stefania Heim

197 **Beyond Imitation** Reverse Engineering the Lyric Poem
Brian Blanchfield

205 **Undressing Advertisements** Poetry as Feminist Critique through
Harryette Mullen's *Trimmings*
Jennifer Firestone

210 **Shadow Poems** Creative Exercises for Revision
Rosamond S. King

217 **The Poem as Divination Tool** The Tarot Card Exercise
Dorothea Lasky

228 **Contributors**

234 **Permissions**

238 **Index of Poems, Poets, and Poetic Forms**

Introduction

While searching for the title to this collection, a poem sprang to mind. It was written by a middle school student at PS 187 in Manhattan where I was a "poet-in-residence" in the spring of 2008. I usually return all original drafts to my students at the end of the residency, but occasionally a stray poem or two stows away in a folder and appears later, too late to return. I like to think this particular piece had a mind of its own, because I've shared it with so many people since its first appearance: an untitled draft scrawled in pencil on college-ruled loose-leaf, no name on the front or back. The prompt was given as the culminating exercise of my year-long program at PS 187: *Write a "poem about poetry" based on your experience so far, using any of the devices we've discussed. No rules — just see what happens.*

Here is the poem, including misspellings and rough edges:

I tell my mother I like poetry
and as the screen glows
She says because it's easy
there's no spelling no grammer
no commas in the wrong place.
You like poetry cuz it's easy, simple
You're lazy she says
her words shatter my ear drums
like the glass of store windows
the shards and splinters lay quietly
in my ears. If I move, they bleed
so I only say no
But poetry is more than easy
poetry is a haven for the demental,
the inormal, the children of lost souls.
Poetry is for those that prefer scrambled eggs
than to sunny side up.
Poetry is for those so eager to be raging and anger
but poetry isn't easy I keep

how is it easy —
to express a thought a feeling
in such few words and phrases
to create a rhythm with no
beat. Poetry is for those without
neat hand-writing
who could never write script
Poetry is the simple spellbound
for those too meager, and insignificant
to speak

Reading it again, I was struck by the line, "Poetry is the simple spellbound." Could it be that "simple" and "spellbound" are adjectives, and the poet omitted a word in the surge to lay down this "mic drop" of a final line? Or maybe this student is using "spellbound" as a noun? Regardless, the line casts a spell of its own. The poem is a refusal and a refutation of the mother's accusation ("You like poetry cuz it's easy"), and the word "spellbound" contrasts with her emphasis on spelling in the opening lines. The speaker rejects the idea that spelling and "grammer" are what matter and offers an impassioned counterargument: poetry is sanctuary, poetry is artful self-expression, poetry is a vehicle for those without a voice.

When we are immersed in the act of writing and not distracted by the clock or self-consciousness or the fear of making mistakes, we are no longer bound to spelling: we are spellbound. This is what I want my students to experience in the classroom when we face our blank pages, pens or pencils in hand. This is what the "lesson" or "prompt" is for: to ease that point of entry, to give an encouraging nudge, and to express, implicitly or explicitly, a sense of play and permission. *Don't worry, see what happens, experiment and explore, this is a just a draft, you're not going to be judged.* When this works, and the majority of the class is writing simultaneously, and I glance up from my own writing and notice that everyone is absorbed in whatever is unfolding on their pages, it is beautiful to witness. And yes, it is a kind of magic.

Intuitively we know that poetry works its magic on our students, even if we struggle to articulate or quantify its specific effects. If people get hung up on the word "poetry" because to them, it conjures rigidity, complexity, rhyme, or meter, then we can call it "imaginative writing." If "imaginative writing" conjures something to be indulged in on the occasional Friday afternoon or during a limited unit, then we can call it "free-writing" or even "pre-writing." But whatever terms we use, our experience tells us that writing in this way has the power to connect students with their brilliance. We witness our students shifting from passivity or dread or deep resistance to a more empowered, creatively engaged position as thinkers and writers.

I don't mean to suggest that teachers are casting spells on their students, zapping them into a trance. I believe the best pedagogical magic of all is to create a space — an atmosphere — in which students can become entranced with their own imaginative abilities. The activities we create, the poems we read or ask students to read aloud, the discussions we lead — all the sequenced steps of our scaffolded lessons — are designed to inspire our students, individually and collectively, to go inward and explore their own potential as writers and creators. We want our students to cast their own spells and to explore the reaches of their minds and imaginations.

My favorite final assignment for a poetry program or college course is to write "poems about poetry." I never ask students to tell me how wonderful poetry is, or how much they've learned. Instead, we might read a selection of other students' examples that I've collected throughout the years, or we simply brainstorm a list of the "tools" that we've learned so far — metaphor, personification, anaphora, etc. — and then I'll set them free to see what happens.

With my college students, I often distribute copies of the kids' responses to this assignment and ask them to find a favorite in the mix — *a poem that you love, that you wish you'd written, or that reminds you of yourself at that age.* One poem that almost always gets chosen is by Nabila, a second-grader:

Poetry, are you losing your
petals? Do you need water?
No, said poetry. Do you need
candy? No, said poetry. Do

you need care? No, said
poetry. What do you need
so your petals don't fall?
I, I need more soil.

That comma between the repeated "I" in the final line —
that hesitation, that sigh — is what gets me every time. Can we
finally agree that, as Keith Haring wrote, art is for everybody? That
every child, every human being is in possession of creativity and
imagination, that this is an essential part of what makes us human,
and that we must cultivate and liberate these qualities rather than
tame or squander them? This book is for everyone who brings (and
sometimes sneaks) poetry into the classroom, knowing that this
"soil" sprouts shoots and flowers. Sometimes even trees. Some
teacher might have done it for us once, and we became spellbound.
May we keep this magic alive and pass it on.

Matthew Burgess
September 2018

How To Use This Book

Spellbound: The Art of Teaching Poetry belongs to a tradition. We see it as a continuation of the Teachers & Writers Collaborative mission, as well as an accompaniment to *Teachers & Writers Magazine* and our other publications. Our motivation for creating this book emerged from a desire to discover, gather, and share some of the newer strategies and approaches that writer-teachers have been developing in recent years. We want to add to the ideas already in circulation, contributing innovative poetry lessons and prompts, especially those that involve contemporary and diverse mentor texts.

This book is intended for writers and teachers who work with students of all ages, from early elementary through college and beyond. We have arranged the contributions in roughly this order — beginning with those intended for very young writers, then gradually increasing complexity until you will find the prompts and lessons best suited for more sophisticated students of writing.

But it is important to note that there are exceptions. Many of these methods can be adapted "up or down" with adjustments, and many of the model texts appeal to kids and grown-ups alike. We want readers to decide for themselves which lessons might work with their students, and we invite you to adapt, change, or create new approaches inspired by something you find here. For this reason, we have not included specific "age ranges" with each piece. You are a better judge of what your students will respond to, and every class of students is different.

In a similar spirit, we opted for a narrative approach instead of a more structured list format. Since making a lesson fly requires more than moving step by step through a sequence, we have invited contributors to reflect on their choices and to include the discoveries they've made in the process. The "art of teaching poetry" involves a balance between intention and improvisation. We plan, but we also remain attuned to what emerges in the moment.

In addition to mentor texts, most of the pieces in this collection include student "model poems." For some young writers, the published poem can feel remote or intimidating. But when you read a poem that an actual student wrote in response — *someone just like them* — suddenly a light goes on and the energy quickens. We encourage teachers to collect their own archive of excellent student work, too. Asking students for permission to share their work with a future class is a great way to validate them as writers while offering a glimpse of their work moving through the world in a larger way.

— MB

What Is a Poem?
Writing Towards
a Wilder Definition
of Poetry

by Erika Luckert

I have many vague recollections of definitions of poetry that were taught to me throughout my schooling, but the description of poetry that I remember most clearly is the one given to me by Lucie Brock-Broido: *a poem is an egg with horses in it*. I remember this definition not because it's clear, or concise, or correct, but because it's wild. A poem is an egg with horses in it. I see the shell, how frail it seems at first, but also the subtle tooth of its surface, its unlikely strength. I hear the sound of tiny hooves tapping at the inside of the shell, pawing at it, pounding at it, clamoring to get out. And I want to write something as wild as that.

The goal of this lesson is not to define poetry, but rather to redefine it — to shift it beyond the expectations of the students and, in doing so, to make poetry a thing that any student might create. I often use this lesson to introduce a poetry program, and it becomes a useful touchstone as we move forward in our learning. Any time a student hesitates over whether something they've written might be considered a poem, I remind them of these definitions, and in them they find their permission to write.

*

I begin the lesson with a simple question: *What is a poem?*

Students give a range of answers — someone might mention that poems rhyme, someone else might say that they don't have to. Someone will probably mention line breaks, or the arrangement of words on the page; they may know the word stanza, or they may not. A student who has paid keen attention throughout English class might mention figurative language or literary devices.

It's only when the room is full of their definitions, of their existing ideas of poetry, that I begin to pass out my own definitions, printed on small paper slips. By now, I've gathered enough definitions that, even in the largest class, every student can have their own.

I ask the students to read these definitions aloud, one by one, until every definition, and every voice, has been heard. Some of the words are difficult — I help the students to be patient with themselves. Some of the definitions are unexpected, or humorous — I encourage the students to laugh, to react.

*

When everyone's slip of paper has been read, I ask them: *How are these different from the definitions you gave me at the start of class?*

As they work through this question, we often land upon the idea of metaphor, and I encourage the students to look back at the definition they have in front of them. *Does anybody have a metaphor?* And we'll read those again, pondering the transformations that are at play. "Poetry is a diary," and I ask what this comparison suggests about poetry. Then we layer in the rest of the metaphor, "Poetry is a diary kept by a sea creature," and talk about how this changes our thinking, building our way up to Carl Sandburg's full definition. "Poetry is a diary kept by a sea creature who lives on land and wishes he could fly." I try to help the students recognize some of their own longings in that sea creature's predicament, to experience the metaphor as something real.

Other times, our discussion centers on the strangeness of many of the definitions. I ask who has a definition that's confusing, or exciting. *Do you agree with the definition you have? Do you disagree?*

All the while, we're opening up our collective idea of poetry, opening it wide enough to include every student in the room.

*

Next, I pass out an index card to each student — there's something about the smallness of the paper that makes it more approachable — and I invite them to invent their own "wild" definition of poetry and write it down. I always ask a few students to share so they can feel each other's creativity in the air.

In some classes, this may be the end of your lesson. If you wish, you might collect the index cards and arrange them together into a collaborative poem.

*

But often, with the stage set this way, we continue, and read a mentor text, a Charles Bukowski poem that in itself answers that question, *What is a poem?*

**a poem
is a city**
*Charles
Bukowski*

a poem is a city

a poem is a city filled with streets and sewers
filled with saints, heroes, beggars, madmen,
filled with banality and booze,
filled with rain and thunder and periods of
drought, a poem is a city at war,
a poem is a city asking a clock why,
a poem is a city burning,
a poem is a city under guns
its barbershops filled with cynical drunks,
a poem is a city where God rides naked
through the streets like Lady Godiva,
where dogs bark at night, and chase away
the flag; a poem is a city of poets,
most of them quite similar
and envious and bitter...
a poem is this city now,
50 miles from nowhere,
9:09 in the morning,
the taste of liquor and cigarettes,
no police, no lovers, walking the streets,
this poem, this city, closing its doors,
barricaded, almost empty,
mournful without tears,
aging without pity,
the hardrock mountains, the ocean like a lavender flame,
a moon destitute of greatness,
a small music from broken windows...

a poem is a city, a poem is a nation,
a poem is the world...

and now I stick this under glass
for the mad editor's scrutiny,
and night is elsewhere
and faint gray ladies stand in line,
dog follows dog to estuary,
the trumpets bring on the gallows

as small men rant at things
they cannot do.

We read "a poem is a city" aloud, often twice, and with
different readers.

How does he describe poetry? I ask. *What kind of city is poetry?
How does he expand his definition of a poem?*

As they talk their way through their reactions to the poem,
students often identify the use of repetition — how Bukowski writes
"a poem is" again and again. I tell them that this repetition can be
called anaphora, and I might even ask a student to count how many
times it happens in the poem.

*

Finally, with their minds limber from all the poetry in the room,
I introduce the writing task. I ask every student to write down
a line at the top of their notebooks — it can be the definition from
their slip of paper, their own definition from their index card, or
even a line from the Bukowski poem. In this way, nobody begins
with an empty page.

Then, I explain that the goal with this exercise is to get their
ideas down on the page as quickly as possible, without stopping to
hesitate over grammar or spelling or what other people might think.
There's no wrong, just write.

The Task: *Begin with the line at the top of your page, and keep
writing. Describe your idea of a poem in detail, give examples, try
metaphors, add more definitions of a poem. If you get stuck, use
anaphora like Bukowski does — repeat yourself!*

*

After about seven minutes of writing, I invite students to share.
We celebrate their creativity by applauding after each reader, and
I comment on the different ways that each student is reshaping
and transforming the definition of poetry.

What is a poem? By the end of the lesson, we don't have
a singular answer to that question, but we've all questioned our

preconceptions about poetry and, what's more, the students have started to take ownership over what they want their own poems to be.

Here are some poems that this lesson has yielded:

A poem about poems

A poem is rain pouring
into a
puddle just beside a
waterfall.
A poem is a plastic bag
blowing in the wind.
A poem is warm coffee
on a cold winter night.
A poem is life in a place
where only death is known.
A poem is happiness
and sadness and everything
between.
A poem is one spoon of
sugar mixed with one pound
of salt.
A poem is the feeling
you get when you cry for so
long that you completely
forget what you were crying
for in the first place.
A poem is the sad cold
brutal truth that I call "my
life."
A poem is the feeling I
get when I am so afraid to be
hurt.

Pilar (7th grade)

Is a Sundae a Poem?

A poem is like having a sundae on a hot summer beach
It does not matter the flavor whether it's apple strawberry or peach
It quenches my thirst in the hot summer sun
Oh! Right now I wish I had one

A poem is like having a sundae in the blazing sun
It makes me happy while I am having my summer fun
It gives me a chill in my throat
It is like a thrill in the summer sun

A poem is like having a sundae any season of the year
Whether it is winter, spring, summer, or fall
An amazing poem inspires us all!!!!

Jayda (6th grade)

The Words of the Heart

A poem is the word of the heart leaking onto the paper
The paper which then tells a story that none have known.

A poem shows all feelings
Happy, sad, mad, or even scared
Trapped up in your heart until it finally leaks on to a paper.

Words so deep
When written you might even feel free
But your heart is the only one capable of telling the story
A poem can force others to see
A story your heart has told
For a poem is the words of the heart.

Jaden (8th grade)

Poetry is

Poetry is like a summer breeze it's like the sun giving you kisses it's like
    drinking hot chocolate in the snow
Like a cool breeze when it's hot
Like a new pencil with a fine point
Like sniffing flowers
Poetry is nice but poetry can be sad and mad and angry
Like stepping on hot concrete
Or being sick
Or yelling so loud that you don't even know what you're saying
Or getting a paper cut
Poetry is our experiences in life our hard times our good times
Our memories our thoughts
It's a way to talk about the things we love and care for
But it's also for the things we hate
Poetry is.

Anise (7th grade)

Resource: Wild Definitions of Poetry

A poem is an egg with horses in it. *Lucie Brock-Broido, quoting a third-grader*

Poetry is an affair of sanity, of seeing things as they are. *Philip Larkin*

**A poem is an experience and not a description of an experience —
a communication of a lively, and even of a rambunctious kind.** *Kenneth Koch*

Poetry is news that stays news. *Ezra Pound*

Poetry is organized violence. *Henri Cole*

A poem is smaller than itself. *Unknown*

A poem is a verbal contraption. *WH Auden*

Poetry is the best words in the best order. *Samuel Taylor Coleridge*

A poem is always married to someone. *René Char*

a poem is a city. *Charles Bukowski*

If prose is a house, poetry is a man on fire running quite fast through it.
Anne Carson

Poetry = Anger x Imagination. *Sherman Alexie*

A poem is solitary and on its way. *Paul Celan*

Poems are handbooks for human decency and understanding.
Elizabeth Alexander

A poem is a message in a bottle to be cast up unto unknown shores.
Unknown

Like a piece of ice on a hot stove the poem must ride on its own melting.
Robert Frost

Poetry must delight and instruct. It must be sweet and useful. *Horace*

Poetry is clumps of words that make people feel something.
Wendy MacLeod

Poetry is truth in its Sunday clothes. *Joseph Roux*

Poetry is just the evidence of a life. If your life is burning well, poetry is just the ash. *Leonard Cohen*

Poetry is an act of peace. *Pablo Neruda*

Poetry is eternal graffiti written in the heart of everyone.
Lawrence Ferlinghetti

Poetry is an echo asking a shadow to dance. *Carl Sandburg*

Poetry is news that stays beautiful. *Yusuf Saadi*

Poetry is everywhere; it just needs editing. *James Tate*

Poetry is frosted fire. *J Patrick Lewis*

I can't remember the meaning of poetry other than it's a broken telephone with which to call the dead and tell them a joke.
Hera Lindsay Bird

Poetry is a diary kept by a sea creature who lives on land and wishes he could fly. *Carl Sandburg*

Finding Your Voices
How Jericho Brown, Diana Ross, and Janis Joplin Can Inspire Student Writing

by Tiphanie Yanique

Why Voice?

When I was a young writer, like in grade school and high school, there was lots of messaging that told me I needed first and foremost to find my own voice as a writer. This felt like a profound social and psychological hurdle — how could I ever know for sure if my voice was original to all of literature; if it was even authentic to an ever-changing me? As I began to read more and write more, I felt that finding one voice was not going to be sufficient for the kind of writing life I wanted. I've come to think that the real task is about finding the voice that is right for the character, poem, story, or what have you — which might mean being able to find not one, but many voices.

Even the dialogue in a piece of nonfiction demands an ability to find nuance in voice for various kinds of people. But how can a writer do this? For me, it's been fun. I don't believe writing should be a tortured experience. I get nosey. I listen a lot. I eavesdrop on conversations. I look at people, how they talk, because a lot of communication is about the body. I also get to know the background of the speaker — or I do the research so I can effectively imagine a speaker's backstory. Because how we talk comes from, well, where we've come from.

This exercise is one I've used across student levels — from elementary to college.

Setting Students Up

Depending on the time we have and the age of the kids, I start by asking them a bunch of questions. I ask about their favorite type of music. I ask what they know about the music. *Where does the music comes from geographically? Historically? What other musical traditions is it in line with? What kind of style is associated with it?* Hip-hop is a good one for this, because most of the kids know the style, and often the teacher in her twenties to forties knows some of the history. It also has so many influences — one student will know that reggae is an influence and another will know about gospel. They can surprise each other, which is always nice.

I then ask the students if they have heard of Diana Ross and Janis Joplin. Somebody usually knows something. Depending on time, I expand off of whatever they know. And then I make the connection, which I have never had a group of students make: *Did you know that they came to fame during the same time period?* It's obvious, but the difference in the work of the two women makes the obvious blurry. So then we talk about the history of the 1960s. We get as deep into that conversation as time, and their age, allows.

Mentor Texts

Depending on which singer the students seem more into, I will start with Jericho Brown's poem where he channels Diana Ross or Janis Joplin. Brown's Diana Ross poem is "Track 4: Reflections." The Janis Joplin poem is "Track 5: Summertime."

Track 4: Reflections *as performed by Diana Ross*

I wanted to reflect the sun.

I wore what glitters, smiled,
Left my eyes open, and,

On the ceiling of my mouth,

Balanced a note as long as God allowed,
My head tilted backwards, my arms stretched

Out and up, I kept praying,

If the red sun rising makes a sound,
Let my voice be that sound.

I could hear the sun sing in 1968.

I learned the word *assassin*
And watched cities burn.

Got another #1 and somebody

Set Detroit on fire. That was power —
White folks looking at me

Directly and going blind

So they wouldn't have to see
What in the world was burning black.

Track 5:
Summertime
as performed
by Janis Joplin
Jericho Brown

Track 5: Summertime *as performed by Janis Joplin*

God's got his eye on me, but I ain't a sparrow.
I'm more like a lawn mower . . . no, a chainsaw,
Anything that might mangle each manicured lawn
In Port Arthur, a place I wouldn't return to
If the mayor offered me every ounce of oil
My daddy cans at the refinery. My voice, I mean,
Ain't sweet. Nothing nice about it. It won't fly
Even with Jesus watching. I don't believe in Jesus.
The Baxter boys climbed a tree just to throw
Persimmons at me. The good and perfect gifts
From above hit like lightning, leave bruises.
So I lied — I believe, but I don't think God
Likes me. The girls in the locker room slapped
Dirty pads across my face. They called me
Bitch, but I never bit back. I ain't a dog.
Chainsaw, I say. My voice hacks at you. I bet
I tear my throat. I try so hard to sound jagged.
I get high and say one thing so many times
Like Willie Baker who worked across the street —
I saw some kids whip him with a belt while he
Repeated, *Please*. School out, summertime
And the living lashed, Mama said I should be
Thankful, that the town's worse to coloreds
Than they are to me, that I'd grow out of my acne.
God must love Willie Baker — all that leather and still
A please that sounds like music. See.
I wouldn't know a sparrow from a mockingbird.

The band plays. I just belt out, *Please*. This tune
Ain't half the blues. I should be thankful.
I get high and moan like a lawn mower
So nobody notices I'm such an ugly girl.
I'm such an ugly girl. I try to sing like a man
Boys call, *boy*. I turn my face to God. I pray. I wish
I could pour oil on everything green in Port Arthur.

We read one or both poems and talk about what we notice. We
also talk about Jericho Brown himself—a male born *after* the 1960s.
How can he access this woman's voice? Sometimes the students
want to talk about if he has right to do this. We go there, if they want,
but we are fundamentally looking at craft. How does the poem work?

When reading the poems, you might ask students: *What
does it mean in "Reflections" that Ross could "hear the sun sing
in 1968"? What was happening in 1968? What do the indents in
every other stanza do? Do they give you a little visual and auditory
break? Are they distractions? Why does Ross (or Brown as Ross)
put "assassin" in italics?*

*In "Summertime," what is the effect of the poem having no stanza
breaks or indents at all? This poem is peppered with tough words
like "chainsaw," "ugly," and "hack." Why does Brown choose language
like that? What is going on with God in this poem? We can look at
both poems and compare—they both talk about God, they both have
italics—but how are these elements used to different impact and effect?*

After a period of discussion and analysis, we look at a clip of
the diva singing the song that is referenced in the poem. There are
endless clips on YouTube of Janis Joplin singing "Summertime"
and Diana Ross and the Supremes singing "Reflections." I advise,
however, that you look up the clips beforehand so you can pick
the one that most exemplifies the poem to your estimation. I pick
a Ross clip where she and the Supremes are wearing glittering
dresses and performing in front of mirrors. I pick the Janis clip
where her hair is all in her face and her back is turned for part
of the performance.

The students and I talk about how the singer sounds, how
she presents herself on stage. We talk about where they actually

are — the Supremes are often in a studio, whereas Janis is often live outdoors.

After having watched each clip, we look at each poem again. *Where do you see evidence of Diana Ross' physicality in the poem?* It's there in "glitters, smiled..." but also in "Balanced a note as long as God allowed...." It's everywhere in the poem. The fact of her being in a studio is reflected in the line, "White folks looking at me."

When we turn to "Summertime," we can ask the same questions. *How do those word choices ("hack," "chainsaw," "ugly," etc.) reflect how Janis Joplin presents herself on stage? Does she "sing like a man" as the poem suggests? Can you see her hiding her face in the performance reflected there in the line about her acne? What more does the word "please" mean now that you have seen Janis perform? What does it mean to be a white girl vs. a colored boy at this time, and how is that reflected in the poem's lines about Willie Baker?*

I have found that students of all ages, even the middle school and elementary school students, have language and experience from which to talk about the racial and gender politics in both poems and clips.

Writing

I ask the students to think about a person they admire, look up to; or conversely, a person they really dislike and do not look up to. I have them write about what that person looks like, where that person lives, what type of world the student imagines they grew up in. Then I ask the students to get that person talking. Just start them talking and talking. *Given what you know about them and their circumstances, what would they most have to say? How would they say it? Would they pause a lot? Would they curse? Should you consider dashes? Would the person apologize all the time? Would they use exclamation points?*

All of this helps students get out of their own heads (well, I like to use exclamation points, but maybe my grandmother doesn't) and helps them with empathy (that person is the way they are because of some life experiences or circumstances, not by accident). Students regularly tell me that they incorporate this method into all of their writing from then on. Me, too, I tell them.

How Long a Lesson Is This?

I have done this lesson in one forty-minute sitting, over a three-hour class, and over three days. I have also used this as revision lesson, to help students rethink dialogue in fiction or nonfiction. If I only have one short time with the students, I will focus on just one clip and one poem — either Janis or Diana. If I have one long block of time, I can do both readings, both clips, and the writing prompt. If I have multiple days, I do the readings in one, and the viewings and writing in another. In all cases, I give the students time to share and get feedback from me and/or each other. The sharing could be another full day of class, or just the last ten minutes of one shorter class.

When doing the exercise with younger children, it might be effective to have them draw the person whose voice they will be channeling. This will give them something to meditate on while they write. Some kids may also just find the drawing liberating, which can loosen them up for the poetry writing. Here is my seven-year-old son's response. The voice he chose to write from was one type of person he really admires: a ninja. After writing the first draft, he said his poem was missing some of the visual aspects of the ninja's voice. So, he added ninja stars. I think the last symbol is either praying hands or nunchucks.

Ninja Hairbraiding

I am a ninja.   *   *
I wear a black
Pants and a black
shirt and have lots of weapons.*
I can talk, but don't.
Now I am sad. I am crying.
My head hurts.
I am taking deep breaths.
Haaawooo.^

Mosiah McGarrah (age 7)

The Lune Link

Illuminating Classroom Content with Flashes of Poetry

by Susan Karwoska

The students are studying immigration or explorers or Native American cultures. They are studying community or New York City. The subjects change from class to class, year to year. I'm in their elementary school classrooms to teach poetry, but I particularly love the work they create when the lesson I bring in allows them to link to their newfound scholarly expertise, whatever it may be.

In this lesson I call the Lune Link, students use a haiku-like poetic form called the lune and photographs related to their studies to write brief, illuminating "snapshot" poems that make imaginative leaps from familiar content. The lune is a wonderfully simple form — three words in the first line, five words in the second line, and three words in the third line. It's easy for even very young students to grasp, but its brevity also means that every word counts. The goal is to have students shine a light on details in the photos that they find compelling, using their recent studies to deepen and enrich their observations. Here's a lune on climbing Mount Everest written by a third-grader whose class was studying explorers:

Tough spiky snow
Scary wind in the air
Me, like nothing

Eli (3rd grade)

Here's another, by a fifth-grader reflecting on the Manhattan skyline:

New York's going
to sleep, but every tower's
still lit up

Matteo (5th grade)

Both the students and I are often happily surprised to see, in the poems they write, what a little lune-light can do.

I start the lesson by sharing two poems that model close observation. The first is William Carlos Williams' "The Red Wheelbarrow." Before I read it aloud I tell the students a little about the good doctor-poet from New Jersey: how he made house calls throughout the towns he served, often jotting down ideas for poems on his prescription pad as he went about his work; how he believed that the ordinary life and lives he saw in his community were fit subjects for poetry; and how he wrote his poems in the everyday — and uniquely American — language he heard spoken around him: informal, unadorned, direct.

The Red Wheelbarrow
William Carlos Williams

The Red Wheelbarrow

So much depends
upon

a red wheel
barrow

glazed with rain
water

beside the white
chickens

Often the first reaction I get from kids when I finish reading the poem is a kind of delighted confusion. "That's a *poem*?" they scoff. It's not fancy enough, they tell me. It doesn't say anything *important*. But almost all are drawn to the poem's first three words, *So much depends*. Something about these words beguiles them, and presents a kind of challenge, too. A few students might venture that so much depends on wheelbarrows or chickens because of their practical use to us. Occasionally a student might suggest that maybe *noticing* these things — the wheelbarrow, the rainwater, the chickens, the red and the white — is what's important. It's always a bit of magic when this happens.

The second poem I share is Gwendolyn Brooks' "The Bean Eaters." (For very young students, you might want to use a poem from Brooks' *Bronzeville Boys and Girls,* a wonderful collection of poem-portraits written for children about the young people in Brooks' Chicago neighborhood. "Cynthia in the Snow" and "Gertrude" are two good choices for this exercise.) In "The Bean Eaters," Brooks creates a portrait of an old couple from the ordinary, unassuming things with which they have surrounded themselves: the "chipware" and "tin flatware" they use to eat their humble dinner, set on "plain and creaking wood." The poem concludes with a list of things, as if the old man and the old woman to whom they belong are fading into a deeper obscurity even as we read about them; are, in fact, already almost gone, leaving behind nothing but these trinkets, these "beads and receipts and dolls and cloths, / tobacco crumbs, vases and fringes."

Like Williams, I tell the students, Brooks believed poetry should reflect the everyday lives and language and concerns of the people in the community where she lived, which in her case was Chicago's South Side neighborhood. Her poems speak of the joys and satisfactions of daily life, but also of the racial and economic tensions that plagued the residents of this predominantly African-American community. "If you wanted a poem you only had to look out of a window," Brooks wrote in her autobiography. "There was material always, walking or running, fighting or screaming or singing."

The Bean Eaters

They eat beans mostly, this old yellow pair.
Dinner is a casual affair.
Plain chipware on a plain and creaking wood,
Tin flatware.

Two who are Mostly Good.
Two who have lived their day,
But keep putting on their clothes
And putting things away.

The Bean
Eaters
*Gwendolyn
Brooks*

And remembering . . .

Remembering, with twinklings and twinges,

As they lean over the beans in their rented back room that
    is full of beads and receipts and dolls and cloths,
    tobacco crumbs, vases and fringes.

I ask the students about the objects mentioned in the poem, and we talk about what these things might tell us about the old couple to whom they belong. The kids are almost always surprised, once we dive into the details, to see how much information any one of these objects can convey. Those dolls, for instance. *What do they tell us about this old couple?* The first response I get to this question is usually that the old man and old woman must have had a child once, maybe several children. *What does it mean that they still have the dolls now, in their old age?* I ask. It means they miss their kids, the students tell me, picking up on the haunting, left-behind feeling of the poem. Or that they're hoping their grandkids will visit them, a student once offered. Or maybe, as another student once said, they are not the kind of dolls you play with but the kind you keep on a shelf, only for decoration. *Any or all of these things could be true*, I say. *Each detail in a poem is there for a reason, every one a clue to the heart of the poem.*

Once the students have seen how these two poets focus in on the details, it's time for them to try it themselves. Before I hand out the photos I've brought in, I pull one from the stack and explain that we are going to write our poems in the form of a lune. I write it on the board, L-U-N-E, then draw an outline of the form so they can see it. Three lines, with blank spaces where the words will go: three blank spaces, then five, then three.

I hold up the photo I've chosen and ask for a volunteer to give me the first three words, describing something from the picture. *What catches your eye?* I ask, reminding them that we are trying to focus on the details rather than the big picture. *Pick one detail and describe it as well as you can*, I say. The lune is perfect for keeping their observations short and focused because its limited word count encourages such specificity. I fill in the blanks I've drawn on the board with the student's response.

Two more volunteers supply the middle and last lines and there it is: we have our poem.

At this point I hand out the rest of the photographs I've gathered from various online sources. Each has some connection to what the students have been studying. While they are looking at the images I read aloud two lines by the poet Allen Ginsberg, who shared Williams' and Brooks' desire to reshape and redefine American poetry. (It's interesting to note that as a young poet Ginsberg was mentored by Williams, and years later he invited Brooks to speak in a course he taught called African American Poetic Genius.) In a poem called "Cosmopolitan Greetings" that doubled as a kind of manifesto, Ginsberg wrote, "Observe what's vivid / Notice what you notice." I say these two lines again to make sure the students have heard them. The kids like the repetition of "notice what you notice," and it helps them understand when I encourage them to look, then look again, at the details in the photographs in front of them. Try *to see not only with your eyes*, I tell them, *but also with your mind*.

Each photo I hand out is different, and there is inevitably some jostling and comparing, but once everyone settles down I tell them I want them to try to write at least three lunes about their photo before they turn it in for a new photo.

Almost as soon as they put pencil to paper I hear the question I'm expecting. "Does the poem have to be 3 words / 5 words / 3 words?" "Can't we use an extra word or two?" I'm strict about this, at least at the start, because I like how the restrictions of the form force them to rethink what they want to say and how they might say it. Many of the best student poems I've seen written in response to this exercise were born out of the unusual and/or felicitous word choices the form obliges them to make. I also tell them that each line does not have to stand alone, that one can run into the next by using the technique poets call enjambment. Finally, I let them know that if they choose to, they can string together a series of lunes to make a longer poem.

In one class, we look at photos of immigrants taken at Ellis Island around the turn of the last century. The eyes in the images gaze out at us from the sepia-toned past with yearning and apprehension and a welter of other emotions. These women and men, children and infants have just arrived at Ellis Island and are balanced precariously between the Old World and the New, the past and the future. My students, fourth-graders, have been studying immigration and are familiar with the broad outlines of the stories these photos suggest, but I am asking them for something more. I am asking them to look again, to find the details — the mismatched shoes, the torn bag, the expression of boredom or hint of mischief on a young boy's face — that will bring these individuals to life.

My students scrutinize the photos. They study the faces, the bodies, the clothes, the background, and begin to write.

Three dirty kids
sitting on couch, tired, bored.
Where are we?

Oliver (4th grade)

A muffin shape
a torn bundle. Secrets hanging
by a thread.

Max (4th grade)

Everyone is scared
Everyone is staring at something
With great surprise

Ashley (4th grade)

For a third-grade class studying explorers, I bring in some photographs of natural wonders and others that depict moments of discovery: footsteps on the surface of the moon, the Grand Canyon, the cave paintings at Lascaux, and the Titanic in its resting place at the bottom of the North Sea. I ask them to name what they are writing about in the title so that they can focus the lune entirely on their observations.

Imagine you are explorers seeing these sights for the first time, I say to them. *Think about the explorers you have been studying. Perhaps, like some of them, you have simply stumbled upon something amazing. Or perhaps you have been seeking what you are seeing for a long time, have suffered mightily to achieve this goal. How would your emotions color your description of these discoveries? What details can you share that will make these things real to others? How will you describe what you see so that others might see it too? How will you say it so that they will believe you?*

On an Arctic Glacier

Made of beauty
Ice cold water threatening the
warm blue sky

Griffin (3rd grade)

On the Hudson River

Trees like zigzags
The river like stained glass
Maze of nature

Saanika (3rd grade)

On Viewing a Lunar Eclipse

The jealous sun
finally controls the moon
A blue lollipop

Nick (3rd grade)

On Discovering the Wreck of the Titanic

The dead Titanic
The perfect home for fish
Its new passengers

Truls (3rd grade)

On the Cave Paintings at Lascaux

How many hands?
Little carved flecks and dots
Color of sand

Some are dissolving
like a giant hurricane passing
with perfect precision

Swirling and spiraling
A disturbance can be seen
Reaching, not grabbing

Rose (3rd grade)

A fifth-grade class I taught was preparing for a school trip and had been making comparisons between Paris, where they were headed, and New York City, where they lived. I gave them photos of both cities and asked them to write about them by zeroing in on details that previously might have escaped their attention, or that provided a clue to the larger character of either city.

Paris Lunes

Trees of Paris
give their cool shade to

the many tourists

In the sunset
friends going home all talking
with each other

Irène (5th grade)

Those pharmacies everywhere
with their big green crosses
shining in streets

Alexandre (5th grade)

New York City Lunes

Big shiny billboards
with all your ads. You
brighten the dark

Tim (5th grade)

Little cars below
Look! These taxis look just
like yellow ants!

Matteo (5th grade)

The educational theorist Maxine Greene believed that giving children the opportunity to engage with art in the classroom was essential in helping them develop the creativity, imagination, and sense of agency "to challenge expectations, to break stereotypes, to change the ways in which persons apprehend the world." She saw art as indispensable for living a moral life, but emphasized that "the capacity to perceive, to attend, must be learned." In the world my students will inherit, it's clear that the need for these skills is more urgent than ever.

The goal of this lesson then, I want to emphasize, is not to have the students "write what they know." It is, in fact, the opposite: to give them a chance to experience how art and poetry can let them see what they know in a new light.

Ode to This Body Singing
Teaching Yusef Komunyakaa's "Anodyne"

by Aracelis Girmay

Yusef Komunyakaa was born in Bogalusa, Louisiana, in 1947, and as a young boy he watched his carpenter father at work. He would go on to talk about how his father's precision and process (measuring, cutting, shaping) later helped him to think about crafting poems. In a language steeped in Bible, speech, jazz music, and place, Komunyakaa brings memory, image, and gorgeous diction together to create lyrical texts that engage the legacies of war, race, human cruelty, and human survival.

In his poem "Anodyne," Komunyakaa creates a self-portrait that is both ode and catalogue. With short lines (that work like breaths!) and in sentences that are sometimes long and sometimes short, he lists what he loves about his body.

Anodyne
Yusef
Komunyakaa

Anodyne

I love how it swells
into a temple where it is
held prisoner, where the god
of blame resides. I love
slopes & peaks, the secret
paths that make me selfish.
I love my crooked feet
shaped by vanity & work
shoes made to outlast
belief. The hardness
coupling milk it can't
fashion. I love the lips,
salt & honeycomb on the tongue.
The hair holding off rain
& snow. The white moons
on my fingernails. I love
how everything begs
blood into song & prayer
inside an egg. A ghost
hums through my bones
like Pan's midnight flute
shaping internal laws

beside a troubled river.
I love this body
made to weather the storm
in the brain, raised
out of the deep smell
of fish & water hyacinth,
out of rapture & the first
regret. I love my big hands.
I love it clear down to the soft
quick motor of each breath,
the liver's ten kinds of desire
& the kidney's lust for sugar.
This skin, this sac of dung
& joy, this spleen floating
like a compass needle inside
nighttime, always divining
West Africa's dusty horizon.
I love the birthmark
posed like a fighting cock
on my right shoulder blade.
I love this body, this
solo & ragtime jubilee
behind the left nipple,
because I know I was born
to wear out at least
one hundred angels.

I love that Komunyakaa lists what is crooked, misshapen, imperfect. He celebrates his body and the survival of his body. From lips, tongue, and hands to kidneys and bones, he lists parts of his body that are both visible to him and invisible (microscopic and/or internal). He also connects his body to a distant place of origin: "divining / West Africa's dusty horizon." His body is *part* of the world — carried by the world just as it carries the world. He reminds us that a body is also a place by comparing its organs, experiences, and shapes to things we associate with places: there is a storm in the brain and moons on the speaker's fingernails.

Before I share the poem with students, I begin by inviting them to generate a list of places that they love or that they feel close to, such as the beach, library, or their grandmother's home. I find that it's always useful to model, with suggestions from the class, what I'm asking students to do every step of the way. For example, I'll ask for a few volunteers to share one of the places that they've listed and I'll write a few on the board. We then brainstorm details of those places:

**sand   clouds   books   pencils   computers   radio
lemon-colored walls   the smell of fingernail polish**

Again, as a group we'll brainstorm the details that we associate with the places we've written on the board. Then I'll ask them to do this for their own personal places that they've written on their individual papers. I encourage students to consider all of their senses and to bring in as many sensory details as possible. You can make a list and then revise for sensory details. So the brainstorm above might turn into:

**café con leche sand   crying, heavy clouds   books
pencils pocked with teeth marks...**

Then we switch gears a little bit. I might say something like, *I'm going to share a poem with you, but first I want us to take one more mysterious step in a new direction. I want us to think about how the body, too, is a place.* Or I might say, *So now that we've got these working lists, I'd like us to do one more thing before we read the poem.* I might add, *I know we're jumping around, but I promise this will all tie together after we read the poem!* I then share anatomical images of the human body on a projection or as photocopies that can be seen by several people at once. These have included images of the brain, the nervous system, the lungs, bones in a foot. Students name the images that they are familiar with and we discuss the ones they do not know.

Now we read Yusef Komunyakaa's "Anodyne" and discuss how it makes us feel, where it gives us goosebumps, what we observe about the poem. (Its music moves and astounds me every time I read it. Love song, Blues catalogue of trouble, swaggery battle song, record of imperfection and loss.) We spend a long time observing the poem. Then we discuss how it's working, what its projects are, what it's enacting. In particular, I ask students to consider the "spleen floating / like a compass needle, inside / nighttime, always divining / West Africa's dusty horizon" and "The white moons / on my fingernails." We discuss the way Komunyakaa is cataloguing his body and also relating it to place.

Part of what I find moving about this poem and this activity is that it gives students a chance to think about their own bodies, to study (and celebrate!) the details of their particular faces and hands, and to imagine and praise the parts of the body that they can't see. With this in mind, I often give each student a compact mirror (shout out to the 99 Cents Store), but the lesson works with or without the mirrors. If they are using mirrors, I ask students to choose three features from their face, hair, or hands that they can see, and three elements from the anatomy board to work with. If they are not using mirrors you can ask them to choose three features from their hands and three elements from the anatomy board. At first, students often giggle to study themselves while they're in the classroom, but I find that they eventually become very interested. I ask them to study their nails, eyes, skin, teeth, eyebrows, hair — looking for striking or interesting details. Questions you might ask them to consider as they look: *What shapes do you feel/see? What details do you notice? Do you notice veins, marks, squiggles, colors, textures, temperatures? What surprises you? Can you find a detail that you hadn't noticed before?*

Once students have their lists, I ask a few students to volunteer to let the group work with something from their list. As a class, we then try to make compelling metaphors and similes that compare the body to some of the details we've listed on the board. Examples:

the lungs are an opened book

eyelashes dark & straight like tiny pencils

my heart is a red cloud raining red

Depending on the group and timing, or how many workshops I have with the group, I sometimes ask students to make different versions of these metaphors and similes (all on the board, collaboratively) — making them more or less detailed, playing with syntax or sound — as a way to get the group talking about possibilities and revision.

I then ask students to create odes to the body modeled after Komunyakaa's. I ask them to merge the details of their special places with the body details that they've listed.

I love that Komunyakaa connects his body to places far from him (the moon, a horizon). He reminds us that a poem can bring things that are far from each other into close proximity. The lungs might be compared to the moon. The heart might be like the earth's molten layer. I can imagine that it is my great-aunt Adey Zuphan (who tended a cornfield and died eight years ago) planting little rows of hair atop my head.

Another thing I admire and love about "Anodyne" is that in it, Komunyakaa celebrates what is often overlooked or uncelebrated. What a gift to remember that my body, with its crooked, goofy, imperfect parts, is the body that enables me to be. Chances are that my injured toes and my beating heart and my broken tooth and my tilted uterus won't be celebrated by anybody else but me, so I better get to singing.

Poetic Introductions
Three Self-Portrait Prompts to Break the Ice

by Emily Moore

In response to an imitation prompt, one of my students chose to do a close imitation of Adam Zagajewski's "Self-Portrait." He introduced himself through his personalized variations on Zagajewski's lines. I loved how Zagajewski's resolute sentences gave him so many openings, so many chances to share his specific tastes and observations. The next fall, I gave Zagajewski's "Self-Portrait" to all of my high school Poetry Workshop classes, along with my own portrait poem that it inspired, and asked my students to write their own poetic introductions by the end of the week.

To begin, I have students do a read-around of this poem, in which I read the title and first line, then have each student read one line as we go in order around their double arc of desks. It is so wonderful to hear each voice, even more so when we as a class support the students who land on Zagajewski's less pronounceable allusions!

Self-Portrait
Adam
Zagajewski
translated
by Clare
Cavanagh

Self-Portrait

Between the computer, a pencil, and a typewriter
half my day passes. One day it will be half a century.
I live in strange cities and sometimes talk
with strangers about matters strange to me.
I listen to music a lot: Bach, Mahler, Chopin, Shostakovich.
I see three elements in music: weakness, power, and pain.
The fourth has no name.
I read poets, living and dead, who teach me
tenacity, faith, and pride. I try to understand
the great philosophers — but usually catch just
scraps of their precious thoughts.
I like to take long walks on Paris streets
and watch my fellow creatures, quickened by envy,
anger, desire; to trace a silver coin
passing from hand to hand as it slowly
loses its round shape (the emperor's profile is erased).
Beside me trees expressing nothing
but a green, indifferent perfection.
Black birds pace the fields,

waiting patiently like Spanish widows.
I'm no longer young, but someone else is always older.
I like deep sleep, when I cease to exist,
and fast bike rides on country roads when poplars and houses
dissolve like cumuli on sunny days.
Sometimes in museums the paintings speak to me
and irony suddenly vanishes.
I love gazing at my wife's face.
Every Sunday I call my father.
Every other week I meet with friends,
thus proving my fidelity.
My country freed itself from one evil. I wish
another liberation would follow.
Could I help in this? I don't know.
I'm truly not a child of the ocean,
as Antonio Machado wrote about himself,
but a child of air, mint and cello
and not all the ways of the high world
cross paths with the life that — so far —
belongs to me.

Over the years, I've expanded my packet of mentor texts for this poetic introduction to include "Ishle Yi Park is...," which opens the door to lists and images, and, most recently, Chen Chen's "Self-Portrait With & Without," a piece that offers my braver writers a level of emotional permission. Sometimes we read them on the same day as the Zagajewski. Sometimes we read them a little later in the week. If we read more than one model, I'll give students a lovely softball of a question — *Which of these poems did you like best and why?* — and have them pair up for a minute and discuss. I just want them to get a feel for what they like. Zagajewski's lush, full sentences? Park's fragments? Chen's vulnerability?

Next, we read my own introductory portrait poem, one that I've written a week or so before starting school. Having students read my work is not typical, but in this case I want my students to see me in the act of writing, and to see my words read and respected by our classroom the way that theirs will be. I've found that writing alongside my students, both by providing the occasional example and by routinely free-writing next to them, hunched over my own composition book in my own student desk for the duration of each prompt I give, lends a sense of importance to the work we do.

Finally, we write! Some groups can just take off from this point. Other, greener classes may need more specific prompts, for instance, *Try creating your own sentences using a few of Zagajewski's opening phrases: "I live," "I listen to," I read," "I like."* Park-inspired students might title the poem with their own names, then list ten vivid metaphors and objects that capture some of their experiences of the world. Chen-inspired students might try writing a list poem using his title, then filling in their own phrases that begin with the words "with" and "without." I tell students that they are welcome to imitate one of our models closely, to merge approaches, or to write in their own style. There's no way to do this wrong. If the poem tells me a bit about you, you've succeeded!

Most years, I give this assignment on the first or second day of class and collect it a few school days after. Sometimes we take ten minutes to work on our poems moments after reading the models. Sometimes we take a few minutes to chat with a partner about how their poems are developing the day before they're due. On the day that students bring in their final, typed versions, we do some sort of group sharing, too, either through a quick read-around of excerpts or through voluntary sharing of whole poems.

After collecting these poetic introductions, I read each with curiosity, underlining phrases I love. I write a few notes in the margins: *I play ukulele, too! It sounds like you have stories to tell. This memory could be the subject of a future piece of writing.* In my Poetry Workshop class, I also try to comment on places where the student's poetic voice is emerging: *You have an eye for strong sensory details. Keep writing from this place.*

I don't grade these pieces, and for me part of the magic comes from the fact that they exist as ungraded, not-quite-official letters delivered during those first moments of September. In fact, this assignment eventually replaced the introductory letters that used to open my ninth- and tenth-grade composition classes. *Here I am,* each poem says. *I've seen all these things. I have a favorite corner of the library. My sister is sick. I play handball. I moved to this country five years ago. Our cat's name is Shakespeare.*

When I've used this lesson to teach teachers or in other situations involving smaller classes, I've given everyone twenty minutes to write and then come back together to share. Sometimes we celebrate the sharing with "read backs" in which we listeners jot down our favorite phrases as the author reads, then applaud and read a favorite phrase or two back to the author in a "popcorn" format, in which students call out their favorite parts of the poems in no specific order. Again, it's a wonderful opener. *Here we are in this room. We just arrived an hour ago, and now we've written poems! And we are sharing them. And hearing them and being heard. We've broken the seal! Let's see what else we can do with the rest of this time we have together.*

Ishle Yi Park is...

a crushed red cosmos.

a crying stone.

a soldier walking through the ruins of a heart.

amazed at the cruelty of x-lovers.

chin up, head high,

queening up instead of bowing down to that king of grief.

a boxcutter under the tongue.

a walled city.

a sky looted of stars.

a crescent moon cutting midnight.

a rusted Chinese star.

a supernova's sister.

a siren song.

a busted 12-string guitar.

a heron taking flight at dusk to a dim horizon.

a loaded, heavy shotgun.

a collapsed lung.

a mewling cry.

shattered glass in asphalt.

diamond cut eyes.

Ishle Yi Park is...
Ishle Yi Park

Emily Moore   39

quicksand.

down Haruki's well with her demons.

a shivering horse flank in a barn no one remembers.

a 77 VHS cassette korean melodrama.

goddamn wishing her delivery guys worked weekends.

waiting for hate to replace the han.

wondering how to melt dry ice.

deciding it's not worth it.

walking away, not looking back,

hard wind on her face, like the legends

she sings of, lovers on arirang mountain

parting over 10 li of distance & time,

both swearing only

the other

will carry the ache.

**Self-Portrait
With & Without**
Chen Chen

Self-Portrait With & Without

With dried cranberries. Without a driver's license. With my mother's
mother's worry. Without, till recently, my father's glasses. With an A
    in English,
a C in chemistry. With my mother saying, You have to be three
    times better
than the white kids, at everything. Without a dog or cat. With a fish.
With a fish I talked to before bed, telling him my ideas for new kinds
of candy. With a tutor in Mandarin. With the 1986 low-budget live-action
TV version of *Journey to the West*. With Monkey King's quest
    for redemption,
Buddhism through monster-of-the-week battle sequences. With thinking
I've grown up now because I regularly check the news in the morning.
With the morning the children, spared or missed by the child with a gun,
go back to school, make the same jokes they made three Mondays ago
but in a different voice. With the younger brother who is taller
than I am. With the youngest brother who wants to go
to art school. With my mother's multilayered worry. With my brothers,
my brothers. With the cry of bats. With the salt of circumstance.
Without citizenship. With the white boy in ninth grade who called me

ugly. Without my father, for a year, because he had to move away,
to the one job he could find, on the other side of the state. With
      his money,
transferred to my mother. With William Carlos Williams. With the local
library. With yet another bake sale for Honduras in Massachusetts
      suburbia.
With the earthquake in my other country. With my mother's long-
      distance calls.
With my aunt's calls from China, when the towers fell.
How far are you from New York? How far are you from New York?
With the footprint of a star. With cities fueled by scars. With the white boy
I liked. With him calling me ugly. With my knees on the floor. With
      my hands
begging for straighter teeth, lighter skin, blue eyes, green eyes,
any eyes brighter, other than mine.

In the examples below, you'll see my students quoting advice from other students. In the past few years, I've had my departing students write Rilke-inspired "Letters to Young Poets" in which they offer poetry-writing advice to my incoming classes. Recently, I've invited students to include a line that spoke to them in their poetic introductions.

Self-Portrait *inspired by Adam Zagajewski's "Self Portrait"*

I laugh about how
I have bad vision.
I see the world sideways.
Sometimes I seriously contemplate the fate of the world and society
but I turn around and read *The Onion*, watch *The Daily Show*,
Crumple up *The Spectator* and throw my own spitballs.
I love to calculate derivatives, 200-meter splits, punchlines
but I can't calculate emotions so
I run.
I gather my teammates around me and tell them that
We're champions and also that

I love them.
I can reconcile theories and observations of physics, but I can't
	reconcile how
Some look over me when I refuse to drink and "bag," while
Others are uncomfortable when I curse and listen to rap.
Few understand when I seek counsel from Bruce Springsteen and
	Kendrick Lamar.
"Write as if you're talking to your best friend," says Grace
Confusing because to me, all my friends are "best friends," and yet
not one of them knows what I can put on this page.
From Coney Island to Washington Heights, I feel the city's irregular
	heartbeat
Feeding mine.
I often ride in the subways — clogged city veins — and I
Contemplate blackbody radiation, envision hurdle races,
Plan out imaginary conversations.
I still believe in some elusive moment when
Everything will click, dreams come true, happiness prevails (Woo hoo!)
When life happens, I fall but keep chasing that vision.
Am I delusional?
I could cry but

I laugh.

Jacob (12th grade)

A Portrait of Aritri

Between school, commuting,
and hanging out with friends
half my day passes.
I've been at Stuyvesant for
four years now,
some days it feels like 10
And some days it still feels like
my very first day.
I always see a clash

between who I am
and what I am.
I love movies like
3 Idiots, *Main hoon na*, and *Munna Bhai*,
but the rap lyrics of
Eminem, J. Cole and Big Sean
Resonate throughout my head and heart.
Right next to my favorite motivational lyrics
There are three bright faces:
My mother and father,
Who taught me that
        in life you have to persevere
  and struggle but
  you should never give up.
And my brother,
  a banker, a college student, a lazy bum, and
  my most trusted confidant.

I grew up with a bilingual tongue
but didn't know how to use it.
I stutter in English,
I mispronounce things in Bangla,
So I turned to the arts.
Crocheting is how I relax.
It's how I've been able to escape
for the past 10 years.
It's how I feel confident,
I take great pride in showing off all the
hats, scarves, and bags I've made,
and take joy
In the fact that
I
can
do
something
with my own two hands.
Poetry became my love.
Of the many poets I have read and admired,

Langston Hughes
will always be my favorite,
for he understands what it's like
to have a dream,
and to sing America.
My history with poetry
Is long and complicated
and deserves a poem of its own.

I worry over every little thing.
I worry about deadlines,
where to sit when there's no assigned seating
and how my peers react to the things I say.
 Will I come off stupid? Ignorant? Annoying?
But then I remember the words
of Calvin, who said
"This is a place for you to let everything out.
Don't be afraid.
No one will judge you."
I tell myself over and over
again
That these words are true
And no one will care
If my poem is
Bland or dark.
Whether I move my seat till I find the one that feels right,
Or whether I talk on and on about something ridiculous.
I just need to be myself,
I just need to be
Aritri.

Aritri (12th grade)

"Love Is a Big Blue Cadillac"
Using Metaphor to Explore Concrete and Abstract Nouns

by Peter Markus

Perhaps we are here in order to say: house,
bridge, fountain, gate, pitcher, fruit-tree, window —
at most: column, tower.... But to say them, you must understand,
oh to say them more intensely than the Things themselves
ever dreamed of existing.

Rainer Maria Rilke, from "The Ninth Duino Elegy,"
translated by Stephen Mitchell

I.

I believe that poetry and metaphor — let's just call it like it is:
I believe that words! — have the power to shape and change the
things we see.

Many years ago, when I first started teaching creative writing
in the public schools of Detroit, I projected a black-and-white
photograph of a young woman's face onto the pull-down screen.
I asked my students what they saw. A girl, they said. *Yes*. A black
girl, they added. *Good*. She's pretty, one girl pointed out. *Yes*,
I agreed, the two of us seeing eye to eye on this. *I'd say she's
beautiful. What else?* I asked. *Look closer*. I wanted them to see the
things — the smaller details — that make up her face: her eyes, her
nose, her mouth, her skin, her hair. Her nose, someone shouted
out, it looks like an anchor. Everybody laughed. *An anchor? Like
on a boat?* Yeah, she said. Don't you see it? *I don't*, I told her. *Show
me.* The girl stood up, walked up to the front of the classroom, and
ran a pointing finger along this other girl's nose: a line that ran
down from her eyebrow and curved off to the left, then ran down
and curved to the right, the way, it's true, that an anchor on a boat
is often drawn by the hand of a child. Ever since that moment,
whenever I look at the human face — at the nose specifically —
I see an anchor in the middle of that person's face, anchoring my
eyes and my mind to it.

This happened again when I was writing my first novel, *Bob,
or Man on Boat*, when the narrator looked down at the hands of
his father, a man named Bob, and uttered these words about Bob's
hands: "His knuckles were rivers." Ever since, when I look down
at my own hands, when I look at the hands and the lined knuckles

of other people's hands, or when I remember the hands of my own father, what do I see? Yes, it's true: I see rivers.

Here's how I go about teaching students to see what's right there in front of them, what I like to call concrete nouns — the moon, for instance — in a new way. I begin with a quick and basic lesson in, of all things, geometric shapes. I draw first a triangle and ask, *What is this?* A triangle, good. I nod my head. Next I make a square. *What is this?* A square, yes. More head bobbing. Then, lastly, I draw a circle. *And what is this?* A circle. We all agree: it is a circle. It's good for everyone to be on the same page at this point: to be looking at and seeing the same thing.

But then I add, *What else might this circle be?*

And here we begin to build a cluster of things, a messy, word-web of nouns, of potential images, and I stand back and watch the blackboard become transformed into a clear night sky filled with constellations of stars.

This is where the students get to be creative. They get to see whatever else they might see, even things that nobody else might see. This circle also might be: a button on an old man's coat, a monocle, a dog's blind eye, a coin without a face, a clock with no numbers, a wheel on a unicycle, a hubcap, the bottom of a bucket, the top of a top hat, a baseball without stitches, a pond seen from a plane flying high above, a magnified drop of water, the bullet hole that killed my daddy, a hole inside my heart. Yes, these all are actual things that students have said about that circle drawn on the blackboard.

If a student hasn't yet offered "the moon" as one of the possibilities, I might prompt them with a clue or simply add it to the list. Then I pass out a poem by Frank Stanford titled "The Moon."

The Moon

I think it is a ship
    putting out without me
A white horse
    that throws all riders

The Moon
Frank Stanford

And a swimmer who is naked
        who believes she is asleep
It is a rooster
        molting dark feathers in the water
Or a beekeeper who dreams
        someone has found her out in the garden
It is a snake that sheds
        its skin in the riverbed at night
And a schoolgirl weeping
        under a black patch
I know it is only a stone
        everybody keeps a blind date with

After we read about Stanford's vision or version of his truth about the moon, what it might also be — *I mean, who among us knows for sure what the moon is, right? I mean, I've never been there, have you?* — I ask students to pick up their pencils and to speak and break through to their own imaginary truth about the limitless possibilities of the moon.

Think about this, I say. *If our circle on the board were a vast multitude of things, why can't the moon be seen as more than just the moon? If the moon is a circle, maybe it too is a button on an old man's coat, or a monocle, or an eye, a coin without a face, a clock with no numbers.* The list goes on and on. The images and the possibilities here are endless. Students need to be reminded of this. Where else but in a poem can we offer our students such a glorious option?

The Moon

I think the moon is an empty face
with no feeling

or a hole in the floor
that you can hear your echo
with the complete silence around you.

Or maybe it's a ball that floated
away far into space.

Or the letter O
in a word but the rest of the letters drifted away.

I know the moon is a heavy ball
but when I visit I can still hold it.

Kendall (7th grade)

The Moon

I think the moon is a tire ready to be
put on a car

or a cookie that the sky is eating
every day.

I think it's a wheel trying to get to
the other side of the street.

Or an eyeball looking at the most beautiful
thing it ever saw.

I think it's a superhero watching over us
or a ball that a dog is trying to get.

I know the moon is only a rock
shining through the darkness.

Gregory (7th grade)

Through our poetry, I tell them, we can take a thing that we think we know, like the moon, which is a universal object — the same moon is seen by eyes in places as far reaching as Detroit to Paris to New York City to Nairobi — and we can transform it into something else. We think we know the truth about the moon but these poems tell us otherwise. Our words, I want them to know, can change the way people see the world, and maybe even the way we see each other who live together in it. This is the essential lesson that I hope for when I teach.

II.

I also believe that poetry and metaphor can shape and change the way we see what can't be seen: the things, emotions, or ideas in the abstract that we carry around inside us. Love, happiness, sadness, anger, fear, our souls even; that's what I'm talking about.

I begin by posing a new question: *What about the things that can't be seen? Those things we carry around inside us? What about those kinds of truths? A circle, the moon in the sky, the features on a young girl's face — these we can point to and say and name — but what about the invisible? Those things that are universal inside each of us, such as love, fear, happiness, anger, joy, grief — or even something as intangible as the soul?*

After floating these questions into the room, I pass out Mary Oliver's poem "Some Questions You Might Ask."

**Some
Questions You
Might Ask**
Mary Oliver

Some Questions You Might Ask

Is the soul solid, like iron?
Or is it tender and breakable, like
the wings of a moth in the beak of the owl?
Who has it, and who doesn't?
I keep looking around me.
The face of the moose is as sad
as the face of Jesus.
The swan opens her white wings slowly.
In the fall, the black bear carries leaves into the darkness.
One question leads to another.
Does it have a shape? Like an iceberg?
Like the eye of a hummingbird?
Does it have one lung, like the snake and the scallop?

Why should I have it, and not the anteater
who loves her children?
Why should I have it, and not the camel?
Come to think of it, what about the maple trees?
What about the blue iris?
What about all the little stones, sitting alone in the moonlight?
What about roses, and lemons, and their shining leaves?
What about the grass?

In her lyric exploration of the soul, Oliver asks questions such as: "Is the soul solid, like iron? / Or is it tender and breakable, like / the wings of a moth in the beak of an owl?" *Where is the soul?* I ask. *Does the grass have a soul? Can you see it? Touch it? Taste it?* The students all seem to agree, the soul lives inside our bodies. We know it is there, they tell me, even though we cannot see it. *But if you could see it*, I say. *What would it be like? Make me see it*, I tell them, as I often do. *Tell me what you think.*

Once we have brainstormed a list of possibilities on the board, I ask my students to pick up their pencils and create their own metaphors. They can follow Oliver's example by asking a series of questions, or they can write, "I think..." and see where their imaginations lead them. Here is some of what they see when they picture what the soul might be or look like.

The Soul

I think it is a hummingbird singing
with a crowd.

Or maybe it's a polar bear in Iceland
or it's possible it looks like

a smiling pancake
or last but not least

a bird flying

in my brown eyes.

Cheyenne (8th grade)

What Is the Soul?

Is the soul soft
like a fluffy warm
pillow?
Does it smell like
the fragrances of
a flower in perfume?
What does it
taste like? Maybe
strawberry short-
cake?
Does it smell like
a flower or is it
a drop of water?
Is the soul the future
of the past?
Is it like a race car zooming
down the track fast?
What is soul? Maybe my
fate.

Shalaya (6th grade)

How to make the unseen visible is the aim of what we are now seeking. These are feelings, emotions, things that we know live inside us, but how can we shape them into something for others to see, something we might hold in order to better understand what we are actually feeling. That's what poetry offers its readers: something tangible for us to hold onto, even if its subject is something that we couldn't otherwise hold in the palms of our hands.

I can hold a picture of the moon in my hand. I can hold a blue stone. But love leaves me empty-handed. Fear, anger, grief, happiness — when I hold out my open hand for students to see what I am holding, all they see is the hand itself. What the unseen offers us, though, is the opportunity to discover what we don't even realize we might think or know about love, fear, happiness, sadness, the soul. *How do I know what I think until I see what I say?* I often say to students.

The words on the page help us better understand what we are seeing, thinking, feeling. To bring out the invisible in us — let's call it the abstract, an idea, an emotion — through visible language. Moon is concrete. The moon is solid — or so we've been told, right? We can see it, name it, point to it. But love? Happiness? Anger? Grief? The spirit? These are important words that make us who we are. But these words live in the abstract. They're soft, mushy, unspecific. We can't look out the window and point to love, or happiness, or fear. These words can only say so much. They are mired in the question, "Love or happiness or anger or grief according to whom?" In a poem, *the who* is the bringer of that specific truth, that story or poem, maybe we can even call it — dare I say it? — a song.

Here are some songs of love, happiness, anger, that which we cannot see until the poet tells us to see it like this.

My Love

My love is as big as a sun shining in the sky.
When birds are singing to a soul.
When houses start to dance
at the dark quiet moon.

Latishia (3rd grade)

My Happiness

My happiness

is like the sky.
The sky is blue

like the sea
is wavy on
the surface.

Quamari (3rd grade)

My Emotions

My anger is like the king of the jungle
getting ready to pounce on his dinner.

My joy is like the shining star you look
at every night before you go to bed.

My fear is like a little girl curled up
under her covers afraid of the monsters

under her bed. My love is like a mother
looking at her newborn baby. My sadness

is like mourners weeping over the dead.
My sleepiness is like a heat wave

on a summer day. My spirit is like a train
that keeps on going. My emotions make me human.

Candance (7th grade)

We must marry or merge the invisible to the visible. We can make use of metaphor to tap into meaning, to what we are trying to say. Ask a student what love is and they might say, "Love is love," or "Love is when I love somebody," or "Love is when somebody cares." But these words tell us very little about something as large as what I believe love to be.

But when a third-grader writes, "Love is a big blue Cadillac / that never runs / out of gas," then I know that love is something I can count on, I don't have to worry about it — this big blue Cadillac — ever breaking down on the side of the road, even when, the poem continues, "It drives all night / down to Mississippi / to see his wife."

Love goes out of its way, this poem tells us. It drives all night, through the dark. I can see it: this love. I am made to see it — this big blue Cadillac. I am better off from being invited to see and experience love in this way.

Here's that poem, "Love Is a Big Blue Cadillac," in its entirety, written by a third-grader in the public schools of Detroit.

Love Is a Big Blue Cadillac

Love is a big blue Cadillac
that never runs
out of gas. It drives all night
down to Mississippi
to see his wife.
I watch them kiss.
When they kiss
the sun rises
like a gigantic cherry
turning the whole universe
red.

Treshon (3rd grade)

This poem teaches us that love is a powerful, transformative thing. Not just the sky is changed, but here the entire universe is tied to that blue car, and the act of going out of its way, of driving all night, for something as simple as a kiss. But isn't love like this, in its ideal form? Like a string of cans dragging on the road behind it, we are made to see and hear and feel the love inside that car. That's what poetry can do for us. It puts us in someone else's shoes, or driving with them in a car, or sitting in the same classroom, or even looking up at a sky that we all of us share, even though we sometimes seem to forget it.

Inspired by Inkblots

Interpreting Visual Images as a Springboard to Poetry

by Chris Cander

One of my biggest classroom challenges isn't managing disruptions or even engaging reluctant writers. It's convincing my young students that there is no "wrong" when it comes to creative writing. Even by third grade, they're in constant pursuit of the correct answers that will result in high marks and high praise. They look at me skeptically when I tell them they are the masters of their imaginations and that thinking—and writing—differently from their classmates isn't just allowed, but essential to the exploration and expression of their ideas.

In 1921, Swiss psychologist Hermann Rorschach created his famous inkblot test using hand-drawn "ambiguous designs" to assess an individual's personality. When someone describes what they see in the inkblot, they reveal something about themselves and how they project meaning on to the real world. The important feature of this test is, of course, *interpretation*.

For this writing lesson, the inkblots aren't used to peer inside a student's mind, but rather to encourage different interpretations of the same image or idea. One person might look at a blob and see a crab; another might see two hearts fighting. Or conjoined twins holding identical balloons, or puddles after a rainstorm. When we discuss our ideas as a class, something shifts: excitement displaces fear. Suddenly, students want to come up with unique and unusual ideas, and instead of worrying that a different view will be perceived as weird, they're proud of their creativity.

Although I teach third grade, this lesson can easily be adapted for any grade level, from pre-writers to college students.

1. First, I talk to students about the value of individuality. I enthusiastically point out and admire wardrobe examples in the classroom—Ellen's cat-ear headband or Isaac's red shoelaces—and we discuss how those small expressions help us understand something vital about the person wearing them. From there, I shift to discussing the importance of being unique in their writing, and how that helps them communicate their personalities, values, ideas, biases, desires, etc. As always, I remind them that there is no wrong in writing.

2. Introducing the history and sharing one of Rorschach's original inkblots, I ask what they see. Using a large sheet of paper or a SMART Board, we make a list of possibilities. After we have a robust number of examples, I encourage deeper exploration: *Do you see more than one figure? How many? What is the relationship between these figures? Did they just meet or have they known each other for a long time? Why do you think so?*

3. As we continue brainstorming, I remind the students of literary devices such as metaphor, simile, and sensory imagery. I ask them to use one or more in order to elaborate on and extend their suggestions about the inkblot example; e.g., going from "turtle" to "a tired turtle whose brown shell is as rough as the bark on an ancient tree."

Now the fun begins!

4. I hand out white stock paper and acrylic paint and instruct the students to fold the paper in half. Using a small amount of paint, keeping away from the paper's edges, they create whatever design they choose on one side of the paper only. Then they fold it again and press and push the paint around to make their inkblot.

   NOTE: This often gets messy, especially with younger students, so make sure the paint is washable and that there are plenty of paper towels for cleanup.

5. After everyone is settled and their inkblots are ready, I return to a collaborative exercise using my own inkblot as an example. Again, students offer interpretations, often spinning with elaborate details. Thus energized, we shift to individual work.

6. I give students five minutes to write three to six images that come to mind when they look at their inkblots. If they claim to be stuck, I challenge them to rotate the paper 90 or 180 degrees to gain a new perspective.

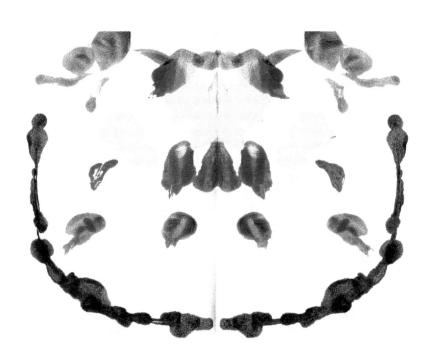

7. Then I give them fifteen to twenty minutes to write a poem or story using their inkblot as inspiration. I remind them again that there are no wrong interpretations, and that since twenty minutes isn't enough time to create a final draft, they should just let their imaginations fly.

Here are some poems written by my students.

The Gods of the Seasons

One day the gods of the seasons had a fight.
They shot flowers that spread out and
Snowballs and leaves.
Their eyes turned white
Then gray
And they faded away into the mists of time.

Victoria (3rd grade)

The World of Melancholy

The days go by with a drooping drag
A million years in a bag of shame
It seemed to be forever until a paint ball hit the wall
The world of melancholy has faded into shadows
A world of sun and flowers appears before my eyes
It smells of clouds, of candy
It seems all good and dreamy
It is all so real
I love this dream
It's great for all to dream

Julia (3rd grade)

The Person

Once there was a person
that had big, beautiful lungs,
but the person was about to die.
She was very sad and the sadder she got,
the less days before she would die.
That day came and when it came,
her lungs flew out of the person and became
a beautiful butterfly.
When that butterfly came out, she
flew up, out, into the sky and soared.
She flew across China, over Japan, and
by California, and went over the world like
never before.
She loved it.
Soon it was dawn and
time to go home.
She flew back from California, and
over Japan, and across China, and soared
to Paradise.
And that Paradise was her home and
she loved it so much.
She was exhausted and as she drifted to sleep,
she said to herself, I am home.
I am home.

*Bell*a (3rd grade)

A Dramatic reVISION
Reviving Revision through Storytelling and Poetry

by Caron Levis

I tell the students to push back their chairs, stand up, and tell each other their life stories...in sixty seconds. The teacher looks ~~horrified~~ intrigued as she watches her thirty or so middle school students talking all at once. I close the door because, admittedly, my lesson on revision is ~~getting loud~~ causing a cacophony — but it's an enthusiastic cacophony; therefore, music to my ears. My objective is to forever replace the typical groans students emit when they're told it's time to revise with the scratching of eager pens — but the busy, shouting, laughing storytellers don't yet know they are currently generating material for writing exercises that will, I hope, re-write their understanding of what writing is. Whether it's fourth-graders in Greenwich, Connecticut, or sixth-graders in Brownsville, Brooklyn — or even my MFA students at The New School University — I hope to let students in on the secret: that for me and most authors I know, writing *is* revision. Or rather, reVISION.

Changing the Language of reVISION

Magic words do exist. By exploring the language we choose to frame tasks for students, we can create an *abracadabra* vocabulary to open minds, make negativity disappear, and summon positive, curious attitudes. For example, in education, the process of *revision* often gets equated with the act of *correction*; the word *correction* implies that you've done something wrong that needs fixing. This can subtly and immediately induce sensations of failure, embarrassment, or shame in students, deflating their confidence, provoking defense mechanisms — and groans. *Go back over your work* hinders enthusiasm because the idea of going *back* suggests a regression; the word "over" is associated with "do over," suggesting we are asking students to repeat a task they've already done and perhaps struggled through. If we want students to be moved to revise, we need language that signals a forward movement, a fresh start. Here are some suggestions to try, edit, and make your own.

reVISION (replaces *revision*): the act of reVISION is where you, the writer, make unique creative choices, express your personality/style, and take control over how you and your work will be presented to the world. This is where you make big choices of structure, length, order, voice, language, rhythm, character, setting, and more. This is being a powerful writer!

Polishing (replaces *correcting* or *fixing*): This is where you make sure your work has its teeth brushed, buttons buttoned, hair combed. This is spelling, punctuation, grammar, handwriting, typos, spacing. This is being a proud proofreader!

"What if...?" is the open sesame to creative thinking. It allows for fresh ideas, imaginative possibilities, big brainstorms. (Replaces *try something different* or *come up with a new idea.)*

"Read your piece with fresh eyes; continue creating by making new choices." (Replaces *go back over your work* or *clean it up, fix things, make it longer, etc.)*

Warming Up for reVISION: An Interactive Introduction to Engage Students

Warning: This activity will get noisy. However, it will be over in about four minutes.

Step 1: Create Partners

Have the students choose A or B. Assure them they will *both* be doing the *same* thing; pairing should be made as comfortable as possible.

Step 2: Instructions

A: Announce, *Okay, for the first round, partner A, you are the Storyteller and B, you are the Greatest Listener Ever. Partner A, you will have sixty seconds to tell B...your LIFE STORY!* Wait for the shocked and confused faces, the "Whaaaat?" Then say, *What this means is totally up to you. There is no right or wrong way, so long as you remain school appropriate. I will put some prompts on the board and walk around in case you need inspiration.* Prompts to put on the board might include (if time allows, ask students to help brainstorm):

- information about my family,
- places I've been, dreams I've had,
- meals I've eaten, feelings I've had,

- languages I speak,
- mistakes I've made,
- subjects I've studied,
- scary memories,
- exciting memories,
- things I'm proud of.

B: Announce, *There are only two rules. Rule 1: Storyteller, you must speak for the entire sixty seconds. Rule 2: The Greatest Listener Ever must be...the greatest listener ever. What will that look, sound, feel like?*

Ask the Greatest Listener Ever to *notice* when they want to interrupt with a "YEAH me too!" or a "Huh?" or "No way!" but *not* to act on it.

Give the listener a simple and specific task, such as telling them that *after* A is done speaking, they will need to tell A one thing, such as: something they'd like to know more about; or one thing they found funny, interesting, striking, or confusing.

C: Ask them to stand in Storyteller and Listener stances. This creates a sense of play and coaxes energy.

Step 3: Go!
A: Using a stopwatch or the second hand on the clock, give a dramatic countdown to *Go!* Use a flick of the light or bell to give them thirty- and ten-second warnings and to signal stop. Instruct everybody to take a deep breath together. Give the Listeners ten seconds to make their observation, instructing A not to respond but to simply take it in.

B: A & B switch roles; repeat above.

C: Now, repeat the cycle but change the time to thirty seconds. Coach lightly with questions such as, *Will you start the same or differently this time? Did your partner's questions give you any new ideas?*

Options: You may do another round at fifteen seconds or one at ninety seconds, or alter the time frame as you feel is appropriate for your students.

Step 4: Reflect and Connect

A: Ask students, *Which time frame was hardest? Easiest? Why?*

B: Validate all answers by pointing out that every writer is unique, and might even experience things differently on different days. One day it might be hard to get started, another day it might be impossible to stop!

C: Ask them to relate the time lengths to different forms of writing: *What are short forms? Long?* (poems, flash fiction, novellas, novels, movie scripts, articles, commercials, greeting cards, etc.)

D: Now ask, *What stayed the same and what changed between your story versions? Why did you keep or change certain things? How? Did you change the order? The content?* Let the conversation evolve and keep a list of the observations on the board, distilling their comments into useful language for revision. (Record and save for future use.) I usually put up a combination of their direct speech as well as reinterpretions of some of their ideas to introduce revision vocabulary. Your list might include:

- Kept what was true.
- Kept what was honest.
- Put things I cared about first.
- Cut out boring stuff.
- Added something I forgot to say.
- Began with a different part.
- Got to the end.
- Clarified, emphasized, re-ordered, replaced, added...

E: Write "reVISION" on top of the list. Ask why the VISION is capitalized. Discuss how reVISION is about thinking big and being creative. Besides writing, when else in life is it important to be able to reVISION something?

Refreshing reVISION: Two Activities to Make Re-writing Exciting

Six-Word Memoirs to reVISION Your Life Story

NOTE: You can call them Six-Word Mottos, or Six-Word Bios.

Step 1:

Announce, *You will now write your life story...using only SIX WORDS.*

Step 2: Model:

Create your own, find some at www.smithmag.net, use the student examples here, or share mine: *Eavesdropping, spying daydreamer writes, erases —, writes... .* Ask students what each author wanted you to know about them. For example, when I read the student example "Running red lights, stopping at green," other students have observed: "He wants us to know that he's a rule-breaker." "He takes risks." "He's unpredictable." "He's dangerous!"

Step 3: Go!

Remind students that, *There is no right or wrong way to do this, only your way.* Validate all writing speeds by inviting them to take time crafting one memoir or trying out several as needed. As a project or ultimate challenge, students can create a poem using Six-Word Memoirs. They'll likely ask if they can use five or seven words; I let them decide for themselves if articles count and encourage them to use punctuation to help shorten. (It's a great way to teach about commas and semicolons.) Student examples include:

Animals and drawing are my life.

Curious, unique, artistic, talkative, beautiful, Russian.

Took the pain and used it.

Like a chocolate chip, semi-sweet.

A path without an accurate map.

Young parents' sacrifice turned out alright.

Dear me, I am better here.

Sophia means wisdom, wisdom means smart.

I am snow and sun bunched into one.

A small raindrop ready to splash.

reVISION the World Poems

Introduce this by showing revision examples of your own work or that of another author to show them how professional writers revise. For example, after a conversation with my editor about an early draft of my picture book, *Stop That Yawn!*, one big reVISION I made was changing the setting from the real-life New York City to the imaginary Never Sleeping City. This opened the story to more fun and created a fantastical world that the illustrator, LeUyen Pham, could really go wild with.

Step 1:

Put previous or newly brainstormed list of revision tactics/ vocabulary on the board. Examples include:

- Find a fresh start.
- Add details.
- Add dialogue.
- Cut words/sentences that don't move the piece along.
- Clarify your meaning.
- Replace dull words with dynamic ones.
- Play with the pace.
- Rearrange sentences.
- Expand a scene/thought.
- Explore a new question.
- Insert an opinion.
- Prove your point with a fact.
- Explore your setting.
- Punctuate!

- Raise the stakes.
- Discover the drama!
- Intensify the climax.
- Put your heart into it.
- Create a moment that echoes.
- Put power in your ending.

Step 2: Model
Share one of the samples below and/or lead the group in creating a poem together using the following steps.

Step 3:
Brainstorm and choose a "juicy" subject. Just as when making orange juice you want to choose oranges that have enough juice to fill the whole glass, when writing you want to choose a subject with enough juice to fill an entire poem or story (e.g., family, siblings, rain, neighborhood, pets, friendship).

Step 4:
Ask students to use one or more pieces of reVISION language as a prompt for each line of the poem. Each line should express what they'd like to change about the topic. For example: "School reVISION: If I could revise school / I would cut out all the bullying / expand recess and art / clarify my homework / substitute the cafeteria with a five-star restaurant / give it a ten o'clock beginning / find an ending that you'll never forget…"

Step 5:
Tell them they each get to write their own "_____ reVISION" poems.

Step 6:
Share!

Here are some student reVISION poems.

World revision

Cut out all the haters
Rearrange some personalities
Bold the love
Underline the importance
Punctuate the fights!
Lengthen the good timesssssss
Backspace the school
Add parties
Strengthen the power.

Ayanna (6th grade)

Relationship revision

If I could revise my relationships with people...
I would CLARIFY who my real friends are,
I would CUT OUT the people who bring me down,
I would ADD more free-spirited people in my life,
I would REARRANGE the choices I make,
I would BOLD FACE the problems I'm gonna have to go through,
and lastly, I would EMPHASIZE that I'm just me!

Chyna (6th grade)

Applying Their VISION: Students Rewrite Their Own Work

Now that you have your students immersed in the language and power of revision, send them to look at their own work, whether it's poetry, fiction, or essay, with fresh eyes and sharp tools. You may want to use these additional ideas:

- Type up first drafts. I've found it greatly enables students to see clearly what their work needs, and revision notes will stand out against the type.

- Structure achievable goals. Using a graphic organizer, notebook, or loose-leaf, have students identify: Something powerful about this piece is _____. When people read my piece I want them to feel _____; think about _____; want to _____ (action). Then have them list one to three reVISION tactics they will focus on; for example, "re-order," "find a strong beginning," "add details," etc.
- Create an atmosphere of concentration: Play some calm music in the background and let them work.
- Partner for polishing: When they have truly finished their reVISIONS, ask them to trade poems with a partner for help with polishing (checking spelling, punctuation, and grammar) to feel like they are checking the mirror to see that there's nothing caught in their teeth. Friends should always, kindly, help each other with spinach and spelling.

NOTE: Add, cut, rearrange, and reVISION this lesson plan as needed to suit your vision. The work is always in progress!

You Are Not You
A Workshop on Ekphrastic Persona and Repetition

by Joanna Fuhrman

I hate the platitude that poetry is "self-expression." If I wanted to "express myself," I'd cry on the subway or write an angry tweet on my iPhone. At its most rewarding, writing poetry provides a way of connecting to something larger, grander than the self; it allows one to experience the glimmering, messy fragments of the self in the gestures and dreams of others. This feeling may be why the poetry lesson I return to the most, whether I am teaching fourth-graders or post-MFA students, is one that asks my students to imagine that they are not themselves. I want them to find "their voice" by giving up the pursuit of it.

To start my lesson, I like to have my students think about the differences between a picture and a poem. *What can one describe in a poem that you can't in a picture? How are visual images similar to and different from poems?* Through Socratic questioning, I ask my students to generate ideas of things left out of a picture. Their answers might include sounds, tastes, movements, a character's thoughts, or passing time. I then hand out reproductions of paintings and ask the students to pick a person — or sometimes an animal or an object — from the reproductions and imagine that they have become this character. I have a wide assortment of reproductions, including work by Van Gogh, William Johnson, Romare Bearden, Jean Dubuffet, and Bruegel.

I give each student a two-page worksheet with a series of questions designed to spur imagistic or figurative language. The questions ask the students to describe not only what they *see* in the picture, but to explore what might be happening in the past or the future, as well as beyond the edge of the image. I try to stress that, unlike worksheets in math or history, there are no right or wrong answers. They should use their imagination to fill in the blanks.

The questions change somewhat depending on the level of the students. I want the questions to challenge them without tripping them up. I always tell my students that if they get stuck on a question, they should skip it for now and return to it later. There are usually enough questions that if the students are not able to finish all of them in the twenty or so allotted minutes, they will still have enough raw material to use as the basis of a poem. While the students are writing, I circle around and encourage them to add more detail to their answers. For example, if the students say they see "food," I'll ask them to list all the particular foods they see.

My questions begin by focusing on the five senses. I start with smell, the sense beginning writers are most likely to overlook, but that Proust reminds us is the most connected to memory. I remind them that when I use the word *you* on the worksheet, I don't mean "you as the writer," but "you as the character in the picture." I leave a couple of inches of space on the worksheet and encourage them to fill it with details. They are, of course, welcome to answer the questions on another sheet of paper if they wish. I often will have to remind them a few times that "you are not you" and write it on the board, as well as the worksheet, as a reminder.

Here are some of the worksheet questions.

1. What do you smell? What does the smell remind you of?

2. What do you hear? What does the sound remind you of? What color would the sound be?

   For less advanced students, I might leave out the third question, which relies on "synesthesia," the blending of one sensory perception with another, such as seeing sounds or tasting words.

3. Describe what you see around you. What is the smallest thing you see? What is the biggest?

   The question about the smallest thing the student sees reinforces the concept of the "close-up lens" I often use when I talk to students about their poems. Instead of asking my students to add detail, I sometimes say, *If you had a camera with a lens that gives you a close-up of an image, what would it allow you to see?* Or if I am commenting on a bunch of poems in a hurry, I might write next to a line, *Use your close-up lens.*

4. What just happened? Did someone say something to another person or thing? Did someone just enter the space? How?

5. What did you dream last night? Again, not you as yourself, but as the person in the picture.

   I add the extra reminder on the worksheet here, because this question is perhaps the most challenging.

6. What is beyond the picture's frame? What is there that we can't see?

7. What will happen next?

8. Fill in the blank: My (part of the body: head, toes, etc.) _____ is (if plural, change verb form) a _____.

   I want the students to experiment with metaphor even if it doesn't make it into the poem. I would only use this prompt with older students.

9. What does the weather taste like? Write a sentence about it.

When most of the students are finished, I hand out "To a Poor Old Woman" by William Carlos Williams and "Infirm" by Gwendolyn Brooks. If there are students whose first language is Spanish, I will also include "To a Guitar" by Federico García Lorca in both the translation and the original Spanish.

To a Poor Old Woman

munching a plum on
the street a paper bag
of them in her hand

They taste good to her
They taste good
to her. They taste
good to her

To a Poor Old Woman
William Carlos Williams

You can see it by
the way she gives herself
to the one half
sucked out in her hand

Comforted
a solace of ripe plums
seeming to fill the air
They taste good to her

Infirm
*Gwendolyn
Brooks*

Infirm

Everybody here
is infirm.
Everybody here is infirm.

Oh. Mend me. Mend me. Lord.
Today I
say to them

say to them
say to them, Lord;

look! I am beautiful, beautiful with
my wing that is wounded
my eye that is bonded
or my car not funded
or my walk all a wobble.
I'm enough to be beautiful.

You are
beautiful too.

After reading the poems out loud, I ask the students what
the two poems have in common. Someone is likely to answer that
both poems include lines that repeat. We then read the Williams

poem again and ask how the repeated line changes. I want students to see that the line break falls in a different place each time. I ask the students how hearing a line multiple times changes how they experience it or feel about it. *How are different words emphasized as they are repeated?* I hope they will answer that the words at the end of the lines sound more important, or that repeating a phrase makes it sound urgent. You might want to introduce the concept of enjambment here, depending on the students' level; talk about how changing a line break can change the feeling and meaning one gets from a line, and say that enjambment is a fancy word poets use to describe breaking a line in an unexpected place. I would then ask them to look at the Brooks poem. *What are the lines that almost rhyme in her poem?*

I try to keep the discussion brief because I want to give them time to write their own poems and share at the end of class.

For the second half of the class or the next class period, I ask students to look at what they have written on their worksheets and circle their favorite lines. They can then use those lines in a poem as is, or they can change them to include in a poem. The worksheet should provide them with raw material for a poem that plays with repetition. I stress that they are free to add additional language to their poems, and need not rely only on their answers on the worksheet.

I am always pleased to see how their poems capture the color, texture, pathos, and surrealism of the paintings their poems arose from. Here are two of my favorites.

Watch It

the tall
   lady in a
   billowing
    gown.

Now it is wearing
 a jacket
 of orange, yellow and
    red.

It is worth
  it to see
  its crown
   of
crystals
  glittering in
the
cold
sunlight.

It catches your
    eye
    with its
    bright green
     hat
    its bright
     green hat
    in the
     rain.

Violet (4th grade)

The Portrait

I was happy, to reach the end of the road
which was freedom.
I enjoy the breeze,
the sun that shines
I see my future wife who in a portrait says *she's happy*
but outside of the supposedly happy portrait
her eyes scream out
I'm not happy!
I'm not happy!
And I never will be!
That was the last portrait that was drawn of us. It was
when we were known
but now we are unknown to the world

trying to create a utopia

but the utopia you think you see is actually the worst utopia

born

trying to jump back in the portrait

and reach happiness, to figure out my mistake

to not end up where I am now

alone, forgotten, and thrown away.

I can always remember that happy day

but every time I notice the picture on the

wall

she jumps out of the picture on the

wall

she jumps out of the picture

and yells everything

again

I'm not happy!

I'm not happy!

and I never will be!

Ariel (8th grade)

"Hanging Fire"
Using Repetition to Write Poems about the Past

by Jasminne Mendez

Students are usually first introduced to, or have a general understanding of, poetry through music and song lyrics. One of the most basic and frequently used devices in both poetry and music is repetition. The song "100 years" by Five for Fighting and the poem "Hanging Fire" by Audre Lorde are clear examples of how repetition can be used to effectively convey the tone, mood, or theme of a piece of poetry or song. The language and subject matter of both pieces are accessible to students because they deal with the teenage years and the struggles, insecurities, joys, and fears students may face.

Oftentimes when we introduce poetry to young students, their first reaction is apprehension. They often say they "can't" write poetry, have nothing to write about, or insist that writing and understanding poetry is "too hard." This lesson allows students to draw from their own memories and experiences to write a poem using a fundamental but potentially powerful poetic device. This lesson can be taught at almost any young adult level and will provide students with the opportunity to experiment and play with repetition in their poetry in order to better convey the mood, tone, or theme of a piece. Whether students are new to poetry or seasoned writers, the writing prompt for this lesson can yield incredible and inspiring results.

Pre-Writing Activities

I like to introduce this lesson by playing the song "100 Years" by Five for Fighting. I first hand out copies of the lyrics to the song or project them on a screen for students to follow along. Before students listen to the song, I ask them to pay attention to what is repeated and what the theme/subject of the song is. I usually play the song twice, since students will notice different lines and ideas each time.

In small groups or as a whole class, I have students discuss what they heard, what was repeated, and what images stood out to them. If the discussion is in small groups, I like to debrief as a class after a few minutes to synthesize ideas from the whole group. Students usually identify that the song is about aging, memories, and how we spend our time here on Earth. At this point I make the connection that like song lyrics, poetry uses repetition. I ask students questions about the effect of the repetition on the listener, and why the songwriter would choose these words or phrases.

After this in-depth discussion, I explain that we will now look at an example of repetition in a poem, and I ask students why a poet would use repetition and how it might influence our reading or understanding of a poem. I hand out copies of Audre Lorde's "Hanging Fire" and ask students to read it silently first. Because I believe that a poem is best understood when it is heard aloud, we then read the poem together and discuss what it is about and the overall tone and mood of the piece.

Hanging Fire
Audre Lorde

Hanging Fire

I am fourteen
and my skin has betrayed me
the boy I cannot live without
still sucks his thumb
in secret
how come my knees are
always so ashy
what if I die
before morning
and momma's in the bedroom
with the door closed.

I have to learn how to dance
in time for the next party
my room is too small for me
suppose I die before graduation
they will sing sad melodies
but finally
tell the truth about me
There is nothing I want to do
and too much
that has to be done
and momma's in the bedroom
with the door closed.

Nobody even stops to think
about my side of it
I should have been on Math Team
my marks were better than his
why do I have to be
the one
wearing braces
I have nothing to wear tomorrow
will I live long enough
to grow up
and momma's in the bedroom
with the door closed.

In small groups or as a class, I ask students to identify the repetition and what effect it has on the reader. They also discuss if they relate to the speaker in the poem. Why or why not? Other questions I might ask students to consider are: *What is the speaker feeling and thinking? Has the speaker had an easy or hard life? Why does Lorde keep the poem in present tense even though this happened in the past? How does the author use questions to move the poem along? What effect does the speaker's race and/or gender have on her experiences?*

I love to engage students with these types of questions because it can open up some really great discussions about identity, race, class, gender, body image, and other relevant adolescent issues. When students engage in these conversations after reading a poem, it shows them that poetry is relevant and accessible to them.

To conclude our discussion of the poem, I ask students to identify (circle/underline/highlight) the active verbs and strong nouns that Lorde uses to create the powerful images in her piece so that they can begin to read like writers, knowing that writers are very intentional about their language and word usage.

Brainstorming

At this point in the session, I explain to students that they will be writing their own "memory poem" using repetition. I start by asking students to make a list of three or four strong memories, events, or moments from their life. These can be positive or negative. I ask them to identify how old they were for each event as this will set up the beginning line of their poems.

If students are comfortable with each other in class, I like to pair them with a partner and have them share briefly the memories they listed. Or I invite a few students to share out to the whole class. Ask students to choose *one* of the memories to be the subject of their poem and have them list their age, active verbs, and concrete nouns related to that memory. Example:

Memory: the Christmas I had the chicken pox

Age: five

Verbs: shivering, shaking, itching, crying, trembling, sweating, whispering

Nouns: blanket, soup, snow, presents, Santa

Once they have completed these lists, I ask students to consider an image from the memory that could serve as the repetitive phrase for their poem. Students might also want to consider a saying or quote they often heard from a parent or loved one. Examples of repetition for "the Christmas I had the chickenpox" might be "and the snow kept falling on the ground," or "I scratch and I scratch." Whatever phrase they choose should carry some larger meaning or serve to set the tone or mood for the piece.

Writing Prompt

Write a memory poem that begins with "I am (age)____" and repeats a word or phrase at least three times, preferably at the end of each stanza. I point out to students that following Lorde's example in "Hanging Fire," we will use the present tense to help bring the past to life. They should be sure to use active verbs and concrete nouns from the brainstorm list to create powerful images/vivid moments that evoke the tone or mood of the piece. Students can also be encouraged to use questions in their poems like Lorde did, and to cluster images one after the other if it makes sense to do so.

As a wrap-up to this lesson, students can share their poems and have classmates discuss strong images and the effect of their repetition on the poem.

These poems were written by young girls in a lockdown facility in Houston, Texas.

New Orleans

I am five years old
lost my home
People drowning from the water
Everything was stoled
No food in my mouth
No clothes
But I still stayed home

We found
shelter in the dome
The smell of mold in
the air, death all around
us but we don't care
We still stayed home

Will I stay on this bridge?
I see a helicopter
it saved me my young
life so hard. I was broken
so much pain has been
unspoken. To live my life away
from my city it brings my
heart a real big pity. But once
I return once again we'll stay &
it'll never end because
We still stayed home.

I am 15

I am 15
And I left my grandmother's house
Living with my baby's father
Still calling my grandmother for support
Even though I left her house
And Mama passed away when I was one

Running the streets while pregnant
Feet hurting while I'm in the streets
My baby's father trying to figure
Out how we're gonna make ends meet
And Mama passed away when I was one

Every corner I see people selling
Drugs to make ends meet
Calling my grandmother everyday she
Wants me to come home
What should I do? I still haven't planned
A baby shower yet and I need her help
And Mama passed away when I was one

Your Secret Hideout
Poems about Real and Imaginary Childhood Spaces

by Matthew Burgess

As an undergraduate English major, I underlined a passage in Vladimir Nabokov's autobiography, *Speak, Memory*, in which he describes, as a boy, crawling through a dark tunnel between the sofa and the wall. It is a minor vignette in a sprawling book, but it stuck with me. Over a decade later in graduate school, I marked a similar description in Virginia Woolf's memoir, "A Sketch of the Past." "How large for instance was the space beneath the nursery table! I still see it as a great black space with the table-cloth hanging down in folds on the outskirts in the distance; and myself roaming about there... ." These two scenes jostled in my imagination and eventually sparked a dissertation about childhood spaces.

When talking to friends or strangers about my topic, they invariably lit up and began recalling their own childhood fort, nook, or hideout. I was struck by how universal these spaces seem to be, and how willingly people described them. I noticed, too, that memories of these spaces elicit different emotional responses. The small childhood space can be a site of blissful reverie or adventure, but it also can serve as a necessary refuge or safe haven.

While there are many versions, these spaces share a common purpose: within their real or imaginary boundaries, children discover and develop their capacity for creative play. Rather than forcing themselves to fit into the world, they temporarily escape and imagine their own. This is likely why these spaces inspire such terrific student poems.

The Lead-in and Discussion

I've led the following poetry lesson with second-graders and with college students, using surprisingly similar approaches. I begin by handing out (or projecting on the board) Robert Duncan's poem "Childhood's Retreat." An audio recording of Duncan reading this poem is available online at the Poetry Foundation website, and I generally prefer to let Duncan be the first reader of his poem.

Before pressing play, I briefly set the scene. I might share a photo of Duncan (I like to put faces to names for the younger writers especially, so that they can see that writers are actual human beings, often with pets, snappy outfits, and senses of humor) and explain

that he is writing about a secret hiding place — somewhere he went
as a kid to explore and to be alone.

Childhood's Retreat

It's in the perilous boughs of the tree
out of blue sky   the wind
sings loudest surrounding me.

And solitude,   a wild solitude
's reveald,   fearfully,   high   I'd climb
into the shaking uncertainties,

part out of longing,   part   daring my self,
part to see that
widening of the world,   part

to find my own, my secret
hiding sense and place, where from afar
all voices and scenes come back

—the barking of a dog,   autumnal burnings,
far calls,   close calls—   the boy I was
calls out to me
here the man where I am   "Look!

I've been where you

most fear to be."

**Childhood's
Retreat**
Robert Duncan

The first time I decided to share this poem with my second-
graders, I was concerned that the poem's diction and lyricism
might fly over their heads. To my delight, they were enraptured —
even stunned — by Duncan's deep voice suddenly filling their
classroom. No one fidgeted, strayed, or spoke out. They were
caught in the poem's spell for the duration of the reading, and this

has proven to the case with most subsequent classes, too.

With the poem still hovering in the air, I ask a few preliminary questions. Nothing analytical yet — just an initial call for impressions. *Where is this place he describes in the poem? How does this poem make you feel as you listen to it?* Then I read the poem aloud for a second time (with the second-graders), or I ask for a student volunteer to read it (with the older students). I don't want to trigger a hunt-for-clues-and-literary-devices at this point, but I might preface the second reading by echoing Allen Ginsberg's advice: *Notice what you notice.*

One of the things I love about teaching this poem is that Duncan makes several unexpected choices that students immediately pick up on. If a student remarks on the extra spaces between words, I ask, *How do those extra spaces affect our reading of the poem?* "They slow you down," they say. Or, "They bring out the emotion in the poem." Then I might reply, *Can you explain why, or how, that works?* It's not important that students respond with eloquent answers to every question; on the contrary, I want to foster an inquisitive atmosphere with very little pressure to perform or provide the right answer.

Keeping the age of your students in mind, some other questions you might ask include:

- How is the boy feeling as he climbs the tree?
- What are his various motivations or wishes for seeking out this "retreat"?
- Can you think of any differences between a hiding "sense" and "place"? Why do you think Duncan chooses to make this distinction?
- Where does the tense shift in the poem?
- Who is speaking in the final lines — and to whom? What is interesting about this dialogue? What might Duncan be implying here?
- If students notice the two instances in the poem that deviate from the version Duncan read in the audio recording, invite them to speculate about the effects of these revisions (i.e. "boughs" vs. "branches," "the shaking uncertainties" vs. "the shaking uncertainties *of song*").

The goal, of course, is to give students the space to articulate their observations about the poem, to lead them toward those articulations with questions and promptings. If they impress themselves and each other with their insights, terrific! If they stare into space but you can see that their wheels are turning, that's great too. "Close reading" is not the purpose of this lesson, but students are gradually developing and deepening their understanding that writers make stylistic choices, and that these choices can alter and enhance a poem's particular magic.

Getting Onto the Page

Once the discussion of Duncan's poem moves toward a natural conclusion (or sometimes, you might choose to interrupt the discussion at the height of excitement), I pose a personal question to my students.

To the second-graders: *Do you have a secret hideout? Where is it? Who is allowed to go inside? Do you enjoy being alone sometimes? Why?* You can expect many, many hands in the air. The challenge at this point is to sufficiently contain the buzzing energy in the room so that students can transfer it into their poems. A bit of conversation and sharing can inspire young writers, stir them up in a good way; too much can dissipate the energy before pencils have touched the page.

Some students will be ready to write with very little additional guidance, and I encourage these students to be as free as possible. *Write and see what happens. Describe your secret hideout using delicious details.* But some young writers need an extra nudge — something that will push them onto the blank page before they're off and running. For these students, I write or project the following prompts on the board with the understanding that they are suggestions, not a list to tick off:

- Where is your secret hideout?
- Describe what your secret hideout looks like.
- How do you get inside your secret hideout?
- Are there any rules or secret passwords?
- Who is allowed in your secret hideout?

I've noticed that young writers like to exaggerate or imagine their secret hideouts with outrageous or fantastical details. Personally, I don't have a preference between a literal description of a physical space or a fantasy fort. In fact, one of the key points about these spaces is that they permit an inward movement and trigger imaginative flight.

With more experienced writers, I use a different approach. I might start by asking students to briefly free-write about one or more places they used to go, as children or adolescents, to be alone. Often these spaces generate a range of complicated emotions for students, so the atmosphere in the room is quieter and more reflective. After students have identified and located personal childhood spaces, I invite them to share some of their ideas. Students who are still searching will find inspiration in other students' responses and a light will go on. Once we achieve that feeling of collective readiness, I ask students to write quietly for five to ten minutes, sometimes with music playing in the room.

When the individual writing is over, I invite students to read aloud. In my experience, both second-graders and college students will raise their hands. There may be some poets who prefer to keep their secret hideouts secret, but others will be more than happy to invite new friends inside.

Some Variations

For homework, I ask my college students to revise the drafts they wrote in class with some additional instructions, such as: *Consider Duncan's use of enjambment, stanza breaks, and spacing. Make intentional choices about how to position the poem on the page.*

If you have time to expand this lesson across two or more classes, you can include Gwendolyn Brooks' "Keziah," Yusef Komunyakaa's "Venus's-Flytraps," Anne Sexton's "Those Times...," Frank O'Hara's "Autobiographia Literaria," and Marie Howe's "The Copper Beech" or "The Game." Or you can consult a collection of poetry, memoir, and visual art in the anthology *Dream Closet: Meditations on Childhood Space.* Once I discovered the universality of this space, as well as people's readiness to describe their own, I issued a similar "assignment" to some of my favorite poets, writers, and artists and collected them into this book.

My Secret Hideout

My secret hideout is in the Arctic.
I have a pet polar bear that I ride on every day.
I have a password that nobody can guess.
Inside I have money. ($1,000,000,000,000,000.)
You have to go in my jet to get in.
I have guards that chop your head off.
I have zombies that eat your brain.
The final obstacle is a huge snake.
It's like a python but ∞ times bigger.
If you get past all that, your head will be exploded.
I have a vicious band of buccaneers
if you get past that.
If you conquer the pesky pirates,
the room of me will await you.

Frederick (2nd Grade)

My Secret Hideout

In my secret hideout you press a button
and then you see a whole new world
inside of you saying you can come in.
All you have to do
is ride a subway and get a ticket
that says "local express train."
Then you get on and ride
to 604th Street and press
the red button and give
the ticket back then
you will have so much fun
at Central Street.

Alera (2nd Grade)

My Secret Hideout

My hideout is inside a whale.
I first go on my pencil slide.
When I get to the whale
it usually picks up its tongue
it waves to me. When he knows
I'm sleeping he turns off
the light switch in him.
When some aliens come
lasers come from the whale's eyes.
When he swallows me there is
a rollercoaster in his fluid.
When a shark bites his tongue
he slaps them.

Alexis (3rd Grade)

Childhood Spaces

Don't you know
That darkness played my haven
Read the script beautifully
When imagination was new
To me. I skimmed my sleep's
Eulogy and drifted.

Two crutches lunge
Over my bed under
A sheet where my head
Gave my pillow craters.
A frontal lobe Frisbee
Tossing and turning like
Pies by Luigi
Or the clock on my cable box
Tock.

Tickets to my mind's show
Were all mine
As my
Brother watched the dirty tapes
I escaped
From the sheltering world
To my world as my shelter.

Inside my sheer veil was vaster
Than a step from my twin
Onto my cloudy housing tiles
Through the giant metal door
With the twisting gold bulb
And into the concrete streets
That liquor shards made
obsidian.

Diamond Bradley (Brooklyn College)

The Laughing Place

Between two rocks
Sidling the river,
A fort. Laughter
Echoes off upper eaves
Escaping through
The downed tree roof.

I'm a soda jerk,
Working the levers
Of unknown time.
You are a customer
Sharing the news.

The rain leaks through
The thatched roof, trickling
Down, dampening shirts.

The river rises, raging
Against the banks
And over the south wall, soaking
The counter top rock.

There were times I
Went without you.
I had no one to serve, and
Nothing to laugh at.

Adam Gallo (Brooklyn College)

If I Was a Bird

A Lesson in Self-Definition

by Amina Henry

I came up with this lesson while teaching a two-week summer writing course for the Hunts Point Alliance for Children in the Bronx. I was working with a group of teenage girls. Teenage girls, in my experience with them, and in my personal experience as a teenage girl, really struggle to find positive things to say about themselves, or even to say things about themselves at all. Very often, if you ask teenagers to describe themselves, the response is, "I don't know." If you press further, you might get, "I like music" or "I'm kind of lazy." It's actually challenging to describe one's self, particularly in a positive way. Teenagers are discouraged from "bragging" or being "arrogant," and yet it's vitally important to see the good in one's self. This lesson was an attempt to get students to describe themselves and to illustrate the idea that we have the power to define and redefine ourselves constantly. It's also a good lesson for exploring extended metaphor and imagery.

I begin by asking a series of questions aloud and invite students to write their responses in a journal or on sheets of paper. *How are you perceived when people first meet you? What five to seven words do you think people would use to describe your personality? If you had to describe yourself as a bunch of colors, what colors would you be? What kind of brown? What kind of red? Red like a rose? Red like an apple?* If they are having trouble, I might open the discussion so that students can share their first impressions of each other. It is important that each individual has several adjectives listed so that they can use them in their poem.

Now we temporarily set our lists aside, and I distribute the following poem by Diana García. I read it first, and then I ask for a volunteer to read it for a second time.

On the First Day She Made Birds
Diana García

On the First Day She Made Birds

He asked me   if I had a choice
what kind of bird
would I choose to be.
I know what he thought I'd say

since he tried to   end
my sentences half the time
anyway. Something exotic
he thought. He thought
maybe macaw.
That would fit
all loudmouthed
and primary colored
he would think.
(He thinks too much
I always thought.)
But really   at heart
I'm more
don't laugh now
  an L B J
   little brown job
except   except
I'm not the
flit   from
branch
to   branch   type
such a waste
of energy all that
wing flap
and scritch scritch scratch.
Really now
can you see me
seed pod clamped
between my beak
like some landowner,
Havana cigar
clenched
between his teeth?
No   I think   not
I think
green heron.
You ask why?
Personality

mainly.
That hunched look
wings tucked to neck
waiting   waiting
in the sun
on a wide slab of rock
alongside a slow river
like some old man
up from a bad night's dream
where he's seen his coffin
and you say to him
Have a nice day
and he says   *Make me.*
Oh   you want looks
I'll give you
looks:
long olive green feathers
a trace of
iridescence
I could stand
going out   iridescent
chestnut sides and head
a black crown
yes   a crown
something regal
to flash when you get
too close
dark bill   bright
yellow legs
and that creamy streak
down my throat and pecs
good
     not great
but good   pecs
just enough for a quick
hop to the next.
The best part
no sexual dimorphism

male   female

both alike

endless possibilities.

Now that the poem is in the air, I ask a series of questions to initiate discussion. *What words or phrases strike you as particularly interesting? What kind of bird does García's friend think she is? Why does García reject this label? What kind of bird does García consider herself to be? Why does García consider herself to be the kinds of birds she describes? How does she describe her personality? What kinds of details does García give? How does García seem to feel about herself?*

Beyond the delicious imagery of the "old man / up from a bad night's dream" and "iridescent / chestnut sides," I want students to notice how actively García is defining herself and how precise she is with her language. I also want them to become aware of how much García seems to *like* herself. I love this poem because it is both unapologetic and meticulous; there is a deep satisfaction for me in the lines "a black crown / yes   a crown." This poem very eloquently presents confidence without ever, in my opinion, slipping into arrogance. I'm also interested in the idea of choosing to be a *bird* with its connotations of freedom and flight and song.

After a period of lively close reading, I give students the following prompt: *Write a poem that addresses one, some, or all of these questions. Incorporate as many adjectives, or "delicious details," as you can. Include at least one example of onomatopoeia, such as García's use of "scritch scritch scratch."*

- What kind of bird do people think you are?
- What kind of bird do *you* think you are?
- Why are you this bird?
- What can you do as this bird?
- What are the colors of the different parts of your body?
- What sounds do you make?

I usually give students ten to fifteen minutes to work on their poems. After their writing time, students are invited to share their work.

This lesson can be easily modified for younger students. You can show beautiful photographs of different kinds of birds, or invite students to research different birds before reading García's poem. Birds are actually really interesting. I've shown students photographs of birds and it has become an absorbing activity—so many colors, so many shapes and sizes! There are many facts to be learned about birds, such as where they live, what they eat, and whether they migrate or build nests. While working on this lesson plan, I learned that jays are noisy and like to steal; gulls live on every continent and mate for life. Depending on how much time you have, you can sit with birds for a while. You can also encourage students to imagine a new bird, a bird from their imagination. Encourage students to compare themselves to birds both in terms of their physical selves and their personalities; students will often want to focus on the physical—nudge them to go deeper. Writing, after all, should be a kind of revelation.

As writers, it's important to grapple with who we are in the wider world and to define who we want to be. This lesson creates a space for this and hopefully shows that self-definition can be, rather than intimidating, filled with possibility. With this lesson, I hope to show that students *can* be birds, and even further, they can be any kind of bird they want to be.

The Day I Grew Wings

Once, my friends and I
stared up at the trees and
tried to guess what each other's birds would be.
I got a flamingo, peacock, or a swan—
something large, yet aggressive.

I disagreed.

I told them I would, in fact, be a
small bird surrounded by others.
I would fly around,
my beak continuously

opening and closing,
opening and closing.

I knew I belonged

conversing with those of
all species, memorizing their callings,
never sitting,
repeatedly eating.

Now, as my feathers begin to sprout,

my colours and stature
make me look more exotic,
making more and more people
pay attention to me.
My short wings spread, revealing
hidden bright quills —
An everyday bird in high end fashion.

I love being
the center of attention —
social, beautiful, needed. And
the day that cage is left open,

my wings will grow 5 times larger
and there I'll be

carrying everyone's praise on
my shoulders.

Erykah (Age 16)

Blues Poems
Borrowing from Song to Write about What's Wrong

by Sheila Maldonado

This form is one of my tried and true exercises, one I have used with a range of ages that always gets the pens going. It also allows me to play music in the classroom, which is always a game-changer. I usually find the atmosphere of a classroom so rigid, the fluorescent lights and stuck windows, often overly lit, airless places that I am always looking to warm up in some way, to get to a place of intimacy from which students can write. I lower the lights or turn them off in the front part of my classroom when I can, and talk to students about writing from that cozier place. Music in a dim room makes it warmer.

I teach this to college-level students in my introductory creative writing class, but have taught it at the middle and high school level too. I use different examples for the levels, but the shape of the lesson is generally the same.

I tell the students that I am introducing them to a form that has been around for much of America's history, that originates from music as so much poetry does, music and poetry forever married if not cousins at the very least, sometimes married cousins. I tell them the influence of the blues is everywhere still today. I ask them if they know of current musical genres influenced by it. If they don't guess, I mention R&B, rhythm and blues, which still includes the form in its name. I, like many of my students, am from an immigrant family that didn't necessarily listen to the blues or speak English in the household. On occasion, I do get some students with families and grandparents from Virginia or somewhere down south, where many Black students in northern cities like New York have roots, who did expose them to the music growing up. It is a history lesson for all of us too far away in place or time to know where the sound and word come from.

We discuss the origin of blues in the post-slavery South of the US. We talk about what that time meant. I ask them what they know of it. *What years were those exactly?* We talk about the one hundred years between the end of the Civil War and the Civil Rights Era. *Was there really freedom for African Americans after the Civil War? Why did a Civil Rights Era occur if there was freedom?* We get to talking about Jim Crow, the KKK, segregation, and voting rights. All this existed in the era that blues and jazz were created, when the US made its first, most particular music.

I tell them I am about to play a song from the late 1930s. I pass out copies of the lyrics so they can follow along. I tell younger students they might laugh because the sound is so old but it was popular music back in its day. The singer, Lead Belly, was on the cover of *Time* magazine and had quite a few hits. He was in jail and made music like quite a few rappers today. He was a star very long ago. I play "Good Morning Blues" from a link on YouTube, the whole version, including his very long talk before the song that is clearly part of it. I don't show the screen. I have them listen. It is a great song for a morning class, as we all lumber in half dazed from dream and dissatisfaction. Its smart, gentle chorus — "Good morning blues, blues how do you do" — stays with the listener for most of the day.

Good Morning Blues
Lead Belly, transcribed by RR Macleod

Good Morning Blues

[Spoken]
Now this is the blues. Never was a white man had the blues, 'cause nothin' to worry about. Now you lay down at night, you roll from one side of the bed to the other all night long. You can't sleep. What's the matter? The blues has got you. You get up and sit on the side of your bed in the mornin'. May have a sister and a brother, mother and father around, but you don't want no talk out of 'em. What's the matter? The blues got you. Well, you go and put your feet under the table, look down in your plate, got everything you want to eat. But you shake your head and you get up and say, "Lord, I can't eat and I can't sleep." What's the matter? The blues got you. Wanna talk to you. Here's what you got to tell 'em.

[Sung]
Good mornin', blues, blues how do you do?
Good mornin', blues, blues how do you do?
I'm doin' all right, good mornin', how are you?

I lay down last night, turnin' from side to side.
Oh, turnin' from side to side.
I was not sick but I was just dissatisfied.

When I got up this mornin' with the blues walkin' 'round my bed.
Oh, with the blues walkin' 'round my bed.
I went to eat my breakfast, blues was all in my bread.

Good mornin', blues, blues how do you do?
Oh, blues how do you do?
I'm doin' all right, good mornin', how are you?

Lord, a brownskin woman'll make a moon-eyed man go blind.
Oh, she will make a moon-eyed man go blind.
And a jet black woman'll make you take your time.

Good mornin', blues, blues how do you do?
Oh, blues how do you do?
I'm doin' all right, good mornin', how are you?

We talk about the meaning of the word "blues," what it conveys. Sadness, most all of the students say, but it is music too, so it is sadness expressed in a structured, lyrical way. By then, I have talked to my students about other forms of poetry, the various shapes and ways it is made, and I have introduced them to the idea of poetry as a container of feelings that can help you express the inexpressible. The limits, the shapes, allow a freedom to say in a way that works, that provides some release. This particular container, blues, is over one hundred years old and has been evoked by a world of poets and singers and they can use it too.

We talk about structure. *What is the shape of this container? How long are the lines? How do they make sounds?* We count syllables, eight to ten a line, roughly. We notice rhyme and repetition. A three-line stanza, the first two lines repeat generally and the last rhymes with it. I write it on the board. I tell them not all blues poems take this form, but most blues songs do. The students don't have to stick to the form if it is too much to replicate but they should at least be familiar with it. I will go on to show them examples of quite a few blues poems, some that are strict with the form and some that break but keep the repetition and rhythm.

We get to the feel, the content. We discuss what the singer is sad about. It is a general sadness, a general dissatisfaction, a malaise. No one around him makes him happy, not his family, not a woman. No white man can feel this, he begins. The song doesn't quite come out and say what is wrong but it is all wrong. The air is wrong, the morning is wrong, the world is wrong. This is a Jim Crow-era song, nothing is right. I ask the students what is there to be sad about now, what is wrong with the world now. What kind of blues do we have? We brainstorm about what gives us the blues and I write the list on the board as they raise their hands:

the MTA

the president

school

family

work

poverty

racism

the police

love

immigration

We read versions of blues poems from a packet I compiled from an amazing little volume called *Blues Poems*, edited by Kevin Young. You can enter this book at any point and be sucked in by the emotion and mastery of form. The book includes both song lyrics, like Lead Belly's "Good Morning Blues," as well as poems by a wide range of American poets. We start with Langston Hughes, the biggest proponent of the form as poetry. In Hughes' play, *Don't You*

Want To Be Free?, the character of the young man says, "That's what the blues is. Sad funny songs. Too sad to be funny, and too funny to be sad." Hughes stays dark and adult, funny yet strict with the form in poems like "Morning After" and "Too Blue," discussing a bad night drinking and a contemplation of suicide as complex and witty as Dorothy Parker's "Resumé."

We move on to Gwendolyn Brooks, who also adheres to the shape and mixes sass and sadness in "Queen of the Blues." "Now show me a man / What will love me / Till I die / Can't find no such man / No matter how hard / You try." We then look at poems that break with the form, like "Tired" by Fenton Johnson, a prose poem and all-time favorite of mine. It is specific, tragic, and plain, yet lyrical from its first line.

Tired

Tired
Fenton Johnson

I am tired of work; I am tired of building up somebody else's civilization.

Let us take a rest, M'Lissy Jane.

I will go down to the Last Chance Saloon, drink a gallon or two of gin, shoot a game or two of dice and sleep the rest of the night on one of Mike's barrels.

You will let the old shanty go to rot, the white people's clothes turn to dust, and the Calvary Baptist Church sink to the bottomless pit.

You will spend your days forgetting you married me and your nights hunting the warm gin Mike serves the ladies in the rear of the Last Chance Saloon.

Throw the children into the river; civilization has given us too many. It is better to die than it is to grow up and find out that you are colored.

Pluck the stars out of the heavens. The stars mark our destiny. The stars marked my destiny.

I am tired of civilization.

For my older students, including some high school age kids,

I have had the honor of introducing them to "Feeling Fucked / Up" by Etheridge Knight. Like "Tired," it has a sense of anarchy that liberates voices in a classroom. Yes, there might be some curse-laden blues by students that follow it, but they often really need to get it out. I've also read the jazz-inspired "You Know" by Jayne Cortez aloud to the class, the repetition and rhythm of which is often inspiration for the students.

For younger kids — middle school and high school — I have read from *Blues Journey*, a picture book rich in lines and images by Walter Dean Myers, illustrated by his son, Christopher Myers. "Pain will push and poke you, / despair will scrape the bone / Misery loves company, / blues can live alone." It also has a great introduction, timeline, and glossary related to the blues and its place in American art and culture. I inundate students with examples to immerse them in this form and history of which they are about to become part.

I read examples from other student poems depending on time. Middle school examples can have as much of an impact on college-level students as any pieces by their peers. My college classes run seventy-five minutes, so I often have time to fit in a great deal of examples from published and classroom poets. For a forty- to forty-five-minute period in a middle or high school, I might stick to the song, one or two poems from a published poet, and one or two from a student poet.

After they have heard the poems, some of which they or I might read aloud, I try to give students fifteen to twenty minutes to write their own blues in response. We share when they are done writing. Sometimes ten minutes of writing can be enough as this form can click quickly with kids. If they are stuck, they don't have to attempt the original form; they can just repeat "I got the blues" over and over and declare what they have the blues about till they catch a rhythm. I tell them to get detailed and specific, to be inside that moment of blues for several repetitions of the line. They are joining an immense chorus of American artists who have sung and written the blues. They write in and about solitude when they write blues, yet they are not alone.

These poems from some of my students can be model blues poems for students you teach.

Jody

I've got the blues 'cause Jody don't love me no more
I used to be his whole world until he decided to explore
Now I'm just some distant planet occupying his space
And even in my own world he's made me feel out of place

I've got the blues 'cause Jody don't love me no more
Says he's loving someone new
And I love Jody so much I said how 'bout you love two
And I say what I don't know won't hurt me
Just meet me Jody for a rendezvous

I've got the blues 'cause Jody don't love me no more
And God forbid if he never really did
'Cause Jody's got my heart and without him how would it beat
Jody is a part of me without him how could I be complete?

Jody don't love me no more and it hurts to my core
but mama says what's that got to do with the time you've been given
'Cause you out here lovin' Jody and not yourself so you really ain't livin'

Manyah Seisay (City College of New York)

A Motherless Child

A motherless child is bad for business
They'll do you wrong and so no wrong in it
A motherless child doesn't know how to love
So if you fall in love
You better run

A motherless child is me
Heartbroken
Feelings of anger hurt and defeat

I try to understand

I really try to understand
But all I can do
is walk around with a heart full of rage

Angry at the world
I can care less
I just want my mother back
Please God give me a second chance

A motherless child is bad for business
I've warned you
Don't get yourself involved with them

Alexander Dajoel Polite (Borough of Manhattan Community College)

My Blues

Living on autopilot but taking no flight
Living on autopilot but taking no flight
Going through the motions all day and lying awake all night

I've got no time to think but I think all the time
I've got no time to think but I think all the time
My mind spitting syllables and I, I just want to feel alive

I look at the mirror, who's that I don't recognize?
I look at the mirror, who's that I don't recognize?
She mimics me and my uncertainty but she is so full of lies

Autopilot take me home before it's my time to die
Autopilot take me home before it's my time to die
I can't live it up, live it up, flying straight to my demise

Bridgette Feliz (Borough of Manhattan Community College)

The Blues

The blues speaks to my mind
then trickles through my body
finding my soul
I have my own blues
that belong to me
They make me rock back and forth
back and forth
the blues the blues the blues
Make me gaze into the zone
of the music
which accuses my mind
yet loses my mind
like I'm ghost
unspoken words
lost in the notes
of this blues poem
I'm done with the blues
yet the notes live on every day
like a new joke

Erica (10th grade)

Familia Blues

I got the blues
porque no tengo a mi familia
I get so sad when I remember them
Yo nunce pensé
que me fuera tan far far de ellos
quisiera cumplir mi sueño de verlos
pero me doy cuenta
que eso será en muchos años
I got the blues
por no tenerlos conmigo
they were everything to me

pero hay que aprender a decir adios
Maybe in the future
los visitaré
I remember the beautiful times
que mi familia y yo vivimos
Mexico and New York
son muy diferentes
Mi familia también me extrañan
and I miss them

Jennifer (7th grade)

"The Truth" and "first time"
Two Prompts That Invite Emotion and Reflection

by Sarah Dohrmann

Writing, for me, has been all of the things that the literary world usually looks down upon: it's confessional ("too feminine"), emotional, cathartic. I once had a literary agent tell me that I needed to be careful not to make my writing into a form of therapy. She wasn't wrong, but I honestly don't know how *not* to wrestle with emotion when I write. For me it's been the only safe place for emotion.

Not everyone wants to dig into emotional spaces, though. Some teens I work with are pretty much dying to be invited to go deep, while others would rather yank their eyeballs out than "go there." Here are two poems that I use with high school students that offer flexibility: they invite those who want to go deep to dive right in, but for students who are less eager to delve, they also function as models for shifting perspectives in a poem.

The speaker in Ross Gay's "The Truth" lands on a humble truth by using the word "because" as a way to get there, while Reina María Rodríguez heightens concrete and specific details in "first time" as tools to understanding one's place in the world. Both are honest and reflective, and both are narrative, inviting students to tell a story of their own. For students who are looking to have an "aha" moment in their poems, I remind them that the trick is to see oneself *through* writing, or by the act of writing. And that to see oneself, one must be open to all of it — not just the pretty stuff. That's what's best about both of these poems: they demonstrate a humility. They show an openness on the speakers' parts, inviting honesty and reflection.

Before I teach either of these poems, I've spent time in previous sessions discussing perspectives in writing. What I mean by perspective isn't just the nuts-and-bolts differences between first-person singular and first-person plural (though these distinctions are discussed), but what I'm talking about are the broader effects of expanding one's perspective, of trying to see through a wider lens than the one you look through in everyday life. When I share "The Truth" and "first time," the first question I ask my students is how the perspective has been broadened in each poem. *What has the speaker of the poem discovered about him or herself? What happened in the speaker's life that broadened his or her perspective?*

The Truth

Because he was 38, because this
was his second job, because
he had two daughters, because his hands
looked like my father's, because at 7
he would walk to the furniture warehouse,
unload trucks 'til 3 AM, because I
was fourteen and training him, because he made
$3.75 an hour, because he had a wife
to look in the face, because
he acted like he respected me,
because he was sick and would not call out
I didn't blink when the water
dropped from his nose
into the onion's perfectly circular
mouth on the Whopper Jr.
I coached him through preparing.
I did not blink.
Tell me this didn't happen.
I dare you.

The Truth
Ross Gay

After the first read, "The Truth" speaks only to a few teenagers. Some students can't get past how gross it is that the narrator said nothing about the man's "water" dripping from his nose into the burger. They say the narrator should've been fired and somebody should've called the health officials. *I agree that a guy's dripping is unsanitary, but why does the narrator not even blink when it happened? What do we know about the two characters in the poem? Why does Gay choose language like "he had a wife to look in the face"? I mean, why not just say the guy had a wife who expected him to support the family? What's the broader perspective the speaker gained in the poem and how did that happen?*

After we've discussed these questions, we talk about the fact that "The Truth" is about an inaction, not an action. Usually when we read a story, the narrator tells us what he did in reaction to an inciting incident, not what he didn't do. Can any students relate to *not* having done something when others might have? Oftentimes in our culture, we think of not doing something as a sign of weakness, but it wasn't weak for the speaker of "The Truth" not to call out when he witnessed the man's "water" drip from his nose. It was a moment of compassion, an act of kindness. I invite students to think about moments when they, too, quietly didn't act when others might have. But even if a student can't think of a time they didn't do something, it's entirely okay to write about a moment of kindness when they did.

Next, we talk about the repetition of the word "because," and how it can be used as a springboard to help a writer into each subsequent line of the poem. It lulls you. We talk about the shape of the poem, too, how it's an inverted triangle that finally, after many "becauses" lands at one single action — or in the case of Gay's poem, an inaction.

Finally, I ask what the speaker of the poem understands differently after the experience. *How did writing the poem help him to understand himself better?*

Here's what Travis, who was a student of mine in a lockdown facility, wrote in response:

Untitled

Because he had a beef with my friends
Because he had a fight with my friend
Because he chose me out of everyone to
    pull a knife on
Because I woke up the next day not in a
    good mood
Because when I approached him in
    breakfast to speak about the situation,
    he disrespected me
Because even though I left him alone, he
    had the nerve to still talk about me
Because I got tired of hearing his mouth
    run on and on
Because he was trynna humiliate me in
    public

Because I snapped and made his mouth
     stop running for a while to come
Because I should have just went to class
     instead of making my biggest mistake
     ever
Because I turned into a person completely
     out of character
Because the shy and quiet shell that
     covered me for so long finally cracked
Because he continued to embarrass me and
     broke the shell completely
Because my friends were there and I felt as
     if I had to prove myself
Because I stopped and tipped my peak
Because he swung and tried to hit me
Because I swung back and actually hit him
     and my anger was being unfair and
     wouldn't let me stop
Because of all that...
I ended up in hell for three months.

Travis

*

Another poem that demonstrates an opening in perspective, thereby inviting student writers to become honest and reflective, is Reina María Rodríguez's "first time."

first time

we went into a market — they call it a *grocery* — and you can't imagine. fruit brilliant as magazine photos. all kinds of different oranges, grapefruits, mandarins, some tiny clementines with a blue sticker — Morocco — they've come so far...the eggs are painted with colors corresponding to the days of the week you're supposed to eat

first time
Reina María Rodríguez, translated by Joel Brouwer and Jessica Stephenson

them: a different color for each opportunity. i felt dizzy, the gulf between myself and this place seemed insuperable. tears welled up in my eyes, i wanted desperately to flee, to get outside so i could breathe. i wanted to explain to Phillis, the North American who had invited me, what was happening to me. i tried, but she couldn't understand: you have to have felt it yourself: the first time. for the first time my mind had crossed over five hundred years of development at jet speed and arrived in the future, a cold future, its display cases filled with artificial snow and artificial heat. there were a thousand things i never knew existed, a panoply of brand names and gadgets for every purpose. i felt like someone from the stone age, and realized most people on the planet never know the era they're living in, any more than they could know the quantity of living matter in this galaxy that surrounds us, or the milky complexity of the molecules in their own brains, and what's more they don't know that they'll die without ever knowing. i felt terror of that gloss, of the waxed fruit, of propaganda so refined it could dilute the existence of the strange things before my eyes, other sensations: everything wanting to be used up, immediately, licked, tasted, eaten, packaged, mastered. i knew i couldn't stand this avalanche, this brilliant swarm, for long, these rows on rows of distant faces staring out at me from cardboard boxes. i'd seen nothing singular in the place, no unique thing i could separate out from the amorphous mass of texture and sensation. i began to move closer, imagining i walked with those who have never eaten meat or tasted cow's milk, who have never nursed except from the teat of a goat. those who have had only wildflowers to chew when the winter hunger comes. i approached closer still, imagining i walked with the salty ones, who collect their water from the public pipe. my nose began to bleed and Phillis said it was the cold; i knew that wasn't the problem. we were near the seafood display, i moved closer. fish have always aroused in me both horror and desire. i moved closer, like a lost child feeling her way through space toward something of hers that's hidden. i brushed the shells with my fingertips, they were smooth and delicate, but obviously artificial, made to be used once and thrown away. at first touch they might seem real, pearly, perfect, but they're actually plastic, and they've never even seen any sea.

The shift of perspective in Rodríguez's "first time" is addressed directly — her first trip to an American grocery store completely shifted the speaker's perspective on the world from which she comes (Cuba), and it helped her to realize that "most people on the planet never know the era they're living in."

Of course when I teach "first time," my students and I talk a lot about the poem's sensory details. I spend some time discussing the differences between "concrete" and "specific" details ("concrete" details engage the five senses; "specific" details deal in the world of the actual) and I invite students to call out where these appear in the poem. I will often take one line of the poem and rewrite it void of its specificity: "i knew i couldn't stand this avalanche, this brilliant swarm, for long, these rows on rows of distant faces staring out at me from cardboard boxes" becomes "i knew this was too much for me to handle so i freaked." And then we talk about how first-time experiences are so great to write about because often you don't even have the language to name the things you're confronted with for the first time. "These rows on rows of distant faces staring out at me from cardboard boxes" are probably cereal boxes, right?

Sometimes I'll make a list in class of "first-time" situations (first time to do a sport, first time to be at a new school, first time in a new country), but often I don't like to do this group brainstorming because I want students to pursue their initial ideas, rather than rely on a list to direct them.

What I like to emphasize most is that the key to writing the "first-time" poem is that opening or humility that allows the speaker of the poem to have a realization. So I ask students not only to write about a "first time" in their lives, but to be sure to include some inner thoughts at the time the event occurred. I try to tell students not to worry so much about an epiphany at the outset. Usually we don't know the "takeaway" of a situation until we write about it. That's the beauty of writing nonfiction — traumatic or otherwise — it's by writing about an experience that one can learn about it.

Recently I led a creative writing club at an international high school with a group of teens who'd all immigrated to the US, many of them not long before our workshop began. Their experiences of arrival were vastly different, but what they could share were their individual "aha!" moments after settling in New York. To write "first-time" poems was a bonding experience for the group — lots of laughter while folks shared, followed by shout-outs of "me too!" — and for me it was a thrill to hear their fresh perspectives on American culture.

The student poem below was written by a young woman visiting from Argentina who participated in Sarah Lawrence College's High School Writer's Week.

First Time

I had *not* seen that coming. When he'd asked for a kiss, I was confident he'd go for my cheek again. He hadn't. Instead, he placed a short kiss on my lips. I was still processing that. He was staring at me now, probably waiting for some kind of answer, anything, really, but I was still processing. I raised an eyebrow at him, as in, *what's going on*. He kissed me again, and I'd had enough time to close my eyes this time. It was weird. Not *bad* weird, but just undeniably odd. Luckily kissing was a) rather intuitive, b) not that bad. I had expected mouths to taste bad, you know, with the saliva thing going on, so I guess I was pleasantly surprised. It was also pretty short, thankfully, so I didn't have to time to begin overanalyzing the fact that maybe kissing wasn't that intuitive and I was just doing a terrible job. Maybe I was doing a terrible job, or at least, it was very evident that I didn't know what the fuck I was doing, because he pulled out first, and asked: "First time?" "I — uh —, *yeah*," I said. At first I was too confused to be embarrassed. But then I became so nervous that I started speaking in English even though it's not my first language, nor is it the language spoken where I live. It was the equivalent of being in the United States and talking with someone, in English, and getting so nervous I'd start to say, *No lo sé, no entiendo nada, esto es raro, tipo no mal raro, pero raro* to someone who doesn't speak Spanish. He didn't mention my speaking in English, though, but rather continued talking like I was still talking in Spanish. Everything was new and confusing. I made all of the kisses be short. I felt kind of bad about that later, though, still do, because I sort of felt like I had used him, like it didn't matter that it was *him* kissing *me*, but rather that I'd wanted to know how kissing felt. It made me feel even worse, because I did care about this person. When it was over, and he was gone, and I had the chance to finally process, I remember feeling numb. Like it was not real. Like somehow I had fallen asleep on the couch and imagined the whole thing. Eventually, it fell into place: *I had just kissed someone, like, on the lips. And I didn't hate it.* I stood up and went to the bathroom. I looked at myself in the mirror: my hair was frizzier than usual and I became aware of just how flushed I was. I realized that I was unconsciously biting my bottom lip, which was rather plumped, trying to remember what this whole *kissing* thing was like: It was pretty awkward, yeah. Kind of fun, maybe? Like something that gets better when you've had more than one go at it. Better than I'd hoped, and strangely very similar and very different from what I had expected.

All together, just kind of

weird.

Lucía Belén Rovasio Aguirre

The One-Sentence Poem
Capturing the Motion of the Mind

by Jason Koo

I got the idea for this assignment from Ed Hirsch, the author of one of the mentor texts below, and over the years as a teacher I've fleshed it out with more guidelines to help my students get the most out of their writing. Ed taught this assignment toward the beginning of his workshop on poetic forms at the University of Houston's MFA program in the spring of 2000, my first year there as a student. I'd been struggling to write poems before that. I'd gotten overly self-conscious about the writing process, largely because of the influence of classes I took as an upperclassman in college, which focused on writing in forms such as blank verse, the sonnet, and the villanelle. We didn't write much free verse, and while my teachers — JD McClatchy and John Hollander — by no means believed in some dumb dichotomy between poems in free verse and poems "in form," they didn't give us the same structural approach to free verse that they did to forms like the sonnet. In other words, they didn't give us the same kind of creative constraints for free verse. So when I went back to writing free verse after working in more traditional forms, I felt hobbled by the anxiety that I was "playing tennis without a net," as Frost would say.

Hirsch changed all that. He taught a class on poetic forms that began not with blank verse or the sonnet, but with free verse, demonstrating in practice (not just in theory) that writing free verse qualified as writing "in form" just as much as counting syllables or following a rhyme scheme. He showed that there are myriad forms within the larger "form" of free verse that have their own structural patterns akin to those of a sonnet or villanelle, so that simply to call something "free verse" was reductive.

The one-sentence poem is one such form. Before Ed's prompt, I'd never thought that using only one sentence in a poem could be just as challenging a formal constraint as, say, writing ten syllables per line, and just as defining of a poem's movement and expressiveness, even its content. The purpose of the prompt is, at a fundamental level, to get poets to understand how crucial syntax is to the form of a poem, especially when writing in free verse. Ed's sense was that poets paid more attention to formal elements like line breaks and sound and less to what they were doing with their sentences, ultimately using short sentences of roughly the same length in almost every poem. This was true in 2000 and it's even truer today, when many poets don't bother with punctuation at all, largely muting the expressiveness of their syntax.

One of the best examples of the one-sentence poem is Hirsch's own "Fast Break," published in his second collection, *Wild Gratitude*, which is one of the books that made me want to study with him in the first place. I hadn't noticed when I read the poem the first time that it was all one sentence.

Fast Break
In Memory of
Dennis Turner,
1946–1984
Edward Hirsch

Fast Break
In Memory of Dennis Turner, 1946–1984

A hook shot kisses the rim and
hangs there, helplessly, but doesn't drop,

and for once our gangly starting center
boxes out his man and times his jump

perfectly, gathering the orange leather
from the air like a cherished possession

and spinning around to throw a strike
to the outlet who is already shoveling

an underhand pass toward the other guard
scissoring past a flat-footed defender

who looks stunned and nailed to the floor
in the wrong direction, trying to catch sight

of a high, gliding dribble and a man
letting the play develop in front of him

in slow motion, almost exactly
like a coach's drawing on the blackboard,

both forwards racing down the court
the way that forwards should, fanning out

and filling the lanes in tandem, moving
together as brothers passing the ball

between them without a dribble, without
a single bounce hitting the hardwood

until the guard finally lunges out
and commits to the wrong man

while the power-forward explodes past them
in a fury, taking the ball into the air

by himself now and laying it gently
against the glass for a lay-up,

but losing his balance in the process,
inexplicably falling, hitting the floor

with a wild, headlong motion
for the game he loved like a country

and swiveling back to see an orange blur
floating perfectly through the net.

Ed showed how by extending your syntax, especially over the course of a whole poem, you could create incredible tension and excitement and momentum down the page. And this kind of form did two things really well: capture physical movement and capture the movement of the mind, often at the same time, so that the two kinds of movement seemed to mirror each other. Since I began writing poems, I'd always been most interested in how a poem could embody consciousness; the poets I was most interested in, such as Whitman and Ashbery, used long syntactical movements all the time to convey the motion of the mind thinking, as did prose writers I loved like Proust. So this assignment, coming at this particular juncture of my life, was a godsend: it opened a gateway for me to write the kind of poems I wanted to write.

I don't remember the poem I ended up writing for Ed's workshop — it wasn't very good. But after that I found myself writing one-sentence poems all the time to try to tap into my mind thinking or, if not writing poems all in one sentence, launching or deepening or closing poems with a long sentence. It became my favorite move, so much so that after a few years of this I had to work *against* it — using shorter or medium-length sentences — to develop my writing even further. If you look at any of my books, you'll see long sentences in just about every poem and many poems that are a single sentence. I still find that a long sentence is the best way for me to launch a poem, especially if I haven't written one for a while or am having trouble putting an idea on the page; once I feel I've pushed off from shore and am at sea within syntax, so to speak, I feel I've started something.

I like to give this assignment to students at the introductory level, especially as a way of introducing them to free verse. It both pushes them to pay close attention to syntax and punctuation (which they usually don't) and serves as a kind of release from the constraints of counting accents and syllables and coming up with rhymes, as I usually teach free verse after blank verse and the sonnet. But this is a great assignment for any level (as evidenced by my experience in grad school), particularly if you're feeling blocked or that your writing is dead rhythmically. It's a great creative pick-me-up. Focusing on just describing a physical action in one sentence, as Hirsch does in "Fast Break," takes some of the pressure off you to wow yourself (and your reader) with what you're doing; you're doing something (seemingly) basic and mechanical. But as you do this you're getting into a rhythm, and the movement of the poem starts to get the mind thinking; almost always the poem ends up becoming an enactment of consciousness. Before you know it, you're in flight!

Prompt

Write a one-sentence poem that moves fluidly and describes a physical action in detail. This should be a complete, grammatical sentence that exhibits your control over its syntax, not a run-on or an unpunctuated stream-of-consciousness amoeba. The music

and movement and momentum of the poem will largely arise
from your nuts-and-bolts precision over the parts of the sentence.
What this prompt is trying to teach you is how control in making
a poem can paradoxically create a feeling of freedom, even
abandon, in the reader.

Guidelines

- Use first-person perspective
- Speak in the present tense
- Use regular stanzas. I recommend couplets, as Hirsch uses
  in "Fast Break," or tercets, as these are good at building
  movement and help create a sense of regulation and order
  as your syntax stretches out.
- Deliver one stretch in the poem of at least five straight lines
  that are enjambed (not ending in punctuation). This is a
  challenge and will help speed up the poem in a compelling
  way if done well. Notice how in "Fast Break," beginning with
  the second couplet, the poem accelerates in breathtaking
  fashion through thirteen consecutive enjambed lines!
- Pay attention to your verbs. Poets often pay too much
  attention to nouns and adjectives, thinking these are the
  building blocks of images, and not enough attention to the
  quality of their verbs. In an action poem, verbs are hugely
  important; they can make or break a phrase or image. I
  suggest using participles (-ing form of verbs), a favorite
  trick of Whitman's, as these are extremely useful at building
  long sentences and creating energy and momentum. Note
  the great participles in Hirsch's poem — "shoveling" and
  "scissoring" and "fanning out" — that bring the fast break
  to life.
- Use concrete imagery! This is like Creative Writing 101,
  but it never really fails, especially in a poem highlighting
  physical description.
- Embed a turn (or several turns) somewhere in the poem,
  as we see toward the end of "Fast Break" when the power-
  forward "loses his balance" and ends up "inexplicably
  falling" and the poem suddenly takes on an emotion that

wasn't there before, connecting us to the loss (noted in the epigraph) that it is trying to memorialize.

Note: The physical action does not have to be something the "I" is participating in; it can be something observed. The first-person perspective of Hirsch's poem is never explicitly announced; it's buried in the description of the fast break ("our gangly starting center").

Another poem that I share with students as an exemplary model of the one-sentence poem is Terrance Hayes' "Carp Poem." It moves more slowly, more deliberately, than Hirsch's, but the description of the physical action gives way to a broader enactment of consciousness, as the speaker makes more leaps into memory and myth and social commentary as the poem picks up speed. These leaps are great examples of the turns mentioned above: the speaker seeing the orange-colored uniforms of the prisoners triggers a flashback to orange carp in Japan, and the memory of the carp packed tightly together leads him to think of Jesus walking across water.

Carp Poem
Terrance Hayes

Carp Poem

After I have parked below the spray paint caked in the granite
grooves of the Fredrick Douglass Middle School sign

where men and women sized children loiter like shadows
draped in the outsized denim, jerseys, bangles, braids, and boots

that mean I am no longer young, after I have made my way
to the New Orleans Parish Jail down the block

where the black prison guard wearing the same weariness
my prison guard father wears buzzes me in,

I follow his pistol and shield along each corridor trying not to look
at the black men boxed and bunked around me

until I reach the tiny classroom where two dozen black boys are
dressed in jumpsuits orange as the pond full of carp I saw once in Japan,

so many fat snaggle-toothed fish ganged in and lurching for food
that a lightweight tourist could have crossed the pond on their backs

so long as he had tiny rice balls or bread to drop into the water
below his footsteps which I'm thinking is how Jesus must have walked

on the lake that day, the crackers and wafer crumbs falling
from the folds of his robe, and how maybe it was the one fish

so hungry it leapt up his sleeve that he later miraculously changed
into a narrow loaf of bread, something that could stick to a believer's ribs,

and don't get me wrong, I'm a believer too, in the power of food at least,
having seen a footbridge of carp packed gill to gill, packed tighter

than a room of boy prisoners waiting to talk poetry with a young black
        poet,
packed so close they might have eaten each other had there been nothing
        else to eat.

Here is a one-sentence poem from one of my students.

Evening Run

Thump, thump, thump, I can hear
the rhythmic pounding of my feet on the ice-crusted road,

grinding powder into a compact mass which
might be slippery the next day when

some unsuspecting child, carrying
a backpack with books and a computer and

the weight of the world, steps on it, but not
perilous enough to make her pirouette gracelessly unlike

the sheet of ice I avoided by swerving
sharply and mildly twisting my ankle

adding a throbbing pain to the burning
inside my calf muscles and the cramp

in my stomach; but I knew I couldn't stop
or give up or catch the next bus because that

would be a sign of weakness and "We
Do Not Quit," I whispered audibly to myself as I

reached the suspension bridge hanging
hundreds of feet above a frozen river

which in the summer is a torrent of youth, gushing
like the endorphins that were supposed to be gushing

through my veins, just like my therapist said
to heal me without medication because

the depression was mild, he said, (and after all,
I wasn't suicidal, just self-pitying), but

exercise was supposed to cure that, he said, regular
aerobic exercises every other day would

keep the anti-depressants away, and in return
all I had to do was to get out of bed and

run past the snow, past the whistling
wind that made my ears numb and

my nose glow fire-engine red and keep
going, laboriously up stairs and then

flat-out sprinting on level ground, until
the agony became sugary sweet.

Rashmi Rajshekar

"i know i am in love again when"
Sparking Strange Play through Multi-Media Poetry

by Cait Weiss Orcutt

As Marianne Moore writes, poetry "is, after all, a place for the genuine," but isn't it also a spot for strange play? As I move from BA to MFA to (my current space, pursuing) PhD, one fear I have is that I'll lose sight of play in all its forms, strangeness, and poetry. By play, I don't simply mean activities we think of as fun. Fun is wonderful, and I do hope fun is part of everyone's writing practice. When I talk about play, however, I am considering play as an act of both resistance and resilience. This sort of play can be understood as an activity that includes a memory of trauma, while simultaneously offering us alternative havens and imaginary spaces to explore and enjoy. Such strange play as poetry allows us to both review and redesign narratives, characters, power structures, and worlds that don't quite serve us *as is*.

Through Writers in the Schools (WITS) in Houston, Texas, I've spent the past year writing with itinerant young people at the Salvation Army of Houston's Young Adult Resource Center (YARC). I've long worked with extra-academic populations — those who have earned degrees but are no longer enrolled in programs, or those who have never had an affiliation with a university to begin with. However, my experience with WITS at YARC is the first time I've had the chance to appear weekly in a safe resource space available specifically to teens and young adults who are working their way back into the system, assuming they were a part of it to begin with.

In working with these writers, I've had the chance to explore how foregrounding play, in all its permutations, can unlock new poetries. I've found that using a combination of poetry and other art forms allows creativity to flourish with this group and opens up my workshop to all levels of literacy and expression.

One of my favorite model texts to use is Bianca Stone's poetry comic, "Practicing Vigilance." I have long been a fan of Stone's work and find it especially electric in writing workshops. Writers of all backgrounds and ages respond viscerally to the image, then jump right into code-cracking to decipher the piece. The group deploys their metaphor-making/breaking skills to decide what Stone's creation might mean. The image makes the whole piece more approachable, perhaps because our earliest introduction to multi-media texts is often through picture books, cereal boxes, print ads, and billboards. Bianca Stone's work introduces the idea of multi-media art to writers while de-mystifying poetry; in turn, this encourages us to experiment — to play, really — with whatever scraps of stories, real or imagined, we have on hand.

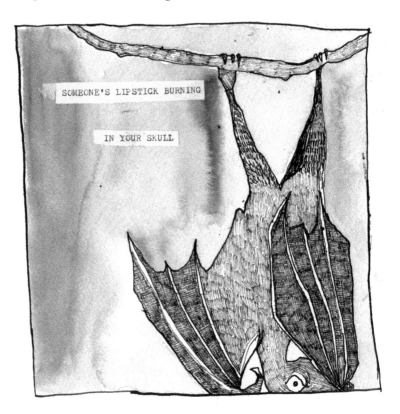

While the text in this work seems focused on romance and obsession ("Someone's Lipstick Burning in Your Skull"), the line also opens up the idea of using art to inspire writing and writing to inspire art. In Stone's comic, our speaker might be the unseen artist (like a voice-over in a film), or it might be the bat anthropomorphically chiming in on its condition. Some playful questions to provoke discussion might include: *How do bats love? Do they have infatuations? Could you imagine a bat in lipstick? If you were a bat choosing lipstick, what shade would you pick? Can you tell a love story entirely from the perspective of an animal? Can you tell one without a single human being involved? Could the bat represent how it feels to hold longing in your brain — memories and fantasies*

flapping around in the dark of your thoughts, causing a ruckus when you know it's time to calm down and go to sleep?

Such questions spark more questions, just as the artwork sparks more writing and vice versa. In considering the love lives of bats, we're challenging genre conventions about what a love story must be. We're opening up our creativity to stories without human characters, stories about nature and animals, love that transcends our culture's stereotypes. In short, through toggling between art and writing in Stone's poem, we're actively sparking strange play.

I enjoy putting poems in conversation, and so, along with Stone's "Practicing Vigilance," I give the writers the poem "i know i am in love again when" by Raena Shirali. I ask a volunteer to read the poem aloud. If time permits, we'll read the poem twice.

i know i am
in love again
when
Raena Shirali

i know i am in love again when

light shakes into the cobwebs woven over
all the empty doorframes. when a nearby car's
bass is a feigned serenade
& the moon seems like a dirty thing. passing
fuselage & hospital lights glint & i'm turned on
thinking they flash for me. me, whose favorite window
features a view that's mostly ground. me,
who's quiet, swaddled, blanket-borne
in the fucking eve, waiting on a call
from my only lover, or a friend six states away.
the space between
saying how much i miss everyone i know
& pressing my forehead to my knee
is usually smaller than i think.
the closest body of water
calls itself a river, but it's stagnant.
i call myself a lot to give, but
that's an exaggeration. walking the bank
i trace ripples — lamp-lit contours that fade
into murk. i am two breaths away from saying
i don't understand happiness

when the voice on the other end of the line
asks if it's okay
to hang up now. what is the opposite
of blank noise? insert that excess
here. i want to live off it.

Once we've heard the poem once or twice, our discussion begins. I focus on Shirali's first lines "i know i am in love again when / light shakes into the cobwebs woven over / all the empty doorframes." *How do you know when you're in love again?* I ask the writers. *If you've never been in love before, how do you think you'll be able to tell when it happens?* Then I ask them to use Shirali's opening line as a springboard into their own poems. Some writers will immediately start filling the page, but others might hesitate. For those hesitating, I try to pull out more ideas. I remind them that "love" isn't just romantic. I ask them: *What beyond humans do you love? The sunrise, the ocean, a dog, chili fries? How do you know you love it? What changes in you when you're around the things, creatures, and spaces you love?*

To help move from discussion to writing, I let the group know I've set a timer for ten minutes. I give a reminder when we get to the halfway point and when there is only a minute left, but if everyone is actively scribbling or sketching once we're at the nine-minute mark, I will extend the time two to five minutes, depending on how long we have left together. I normally circulate during "writing time," helping anyone who seems confused or blocked with questions like, *If love were a color, what color would it be?* or any other encouragement to think creatively or metaphorically about the topic at hand. If students prefer to draw during the "writing time," I will ask them to write one line — a collection of three to ten words — somewhere on the page (a la Bianca Stone's model text).

As a conclusion to the activity, I invite students to share their responses with the group. I may offer brief comments about what is vivid or memorable in their piece, and if other participants want to follow suit with positive feedback, they are welcome. As a result of this lesson, writers who might have walked into the room doubting their creative skills leave having created a fresh poem and/or poetry comic. They've played strangely and "poemed" their way through love and/or heartbreak. They've made a tiny miracle of art and reinvention out of life.

And because they have made something out of a world that so often breaks things apart, we can discuss how art saves us, in its way, and what new possibilities and reinventions become possible when we refuse to keep things separate (writing vs. drawing, human vs. animal, lover vs. beloved) and instead, focus on making connections and communicating our shared and unique experiences on as many levels as possible.

The Poetics of Liberation

Looking Back to Envision the Future

by Alex Cuff

A central question I grapple with as a white teacher working in a predominantly Black and Latinx school community is how to effectively teach racialized content in a way that brings joy and empowerment into the classroom, as opposed to a curriculum that solely centers narratives of pain and oppression as if they are the defining experience of people of color. A great mentor, activist, scholar, educator, and founder of CREADnyc (Culturally Responsive Educators of the African Diaspora), the late Khalilah Brann used to lovingly admonish me, "There needs to be joy in your curriculum, Alex!"

While developing my units for the 2017–2018 school year, I participated in a year-long series of workshops developed by Brann and titled *Woke Cypha*, which aimed to create "learning experiences that are centered in the development and mastery of academic skills and positive racial identity development for students of the African Diaspora." The workshops introduced participants to several guiding principles for developing culturally responsive curriculum for Black and Brown students in New York City, including the Sankofa principle. Sankofa is an African word from the Akan tribe in Ghana. The literal translation of the word is, "It is not taboo to fetch what is at risk of being left behind." The etymology of the word is SAN (return), KO (go), FA (look, seek, and take), and the symbol is a bird with its feet firmly planted forward and its head turned backwards. The principle of Sankofa teaches that a strong future cannot be separate from seeking knowledge of the past.

"Don't scare me like that, colonizer."

"Wakanda forever!" could be heard through the halls at Academy for Young Writers in East New York, Brooklyn, throughout February and March as I began my spring semester writing elective with a group of tenth-graders. I wanted to harness the energy that had spread as a result of Ryan Coogler's film *Black Panther*, set in Wakanda, a technologically advanced African nation that had never been colonized. In April, we began our poetry unit with a brief introduction to Afrofuturism via Wakanda and Janelle Monae's album *Dirty Computer*. Then we started exploring the work of artists whose content and craft invoke liberatory realities, such as Jamila Woods, Eve Ewing, Zoe Leonard, and Adjua Gargi Nzinga Greaves.

The lesson included here is the fourteenth of twenty-three. After spending time considering how poets write alternate ways of being in the world, this lesson introduces students to the concept of Sankofa as a possible framework for writing poetry. The unit's essential questions are: How do poets write liberatory futures into being? How do poets use language to disrupt an unjust world? What language is helpful in discussing a writer's craft? Although I have taught the following lesson within this extended unit, you can adapt it into a stand-alone, two-part lesson that might be used in any poetry, history, or literature course.

Part One: Where Do You Stand?

As an opener, I post the following two statements and ask students to choose the one that most aligns to their own perspective:

A. We cannot change what has happened in the past so we should focus on creating a better future.

B. The knowledge of the past must never be forgotten if we want to ensure a strong future.

I ask students to identify as an "A" or a "B" depending on the statement that resonates most, and have the As and Bs gather at different sides of the room. Once students are in groups, I ask them to share their reason for agreeing with the statement they chose, and then ask them to consider reasons that one might disagree with their perspective. In other words, I ask them to identify a possible counter argument. After approximately three minutes, I invite each group to choose a spokesperson to share their responses. I find by the end of the brief share out, students mostly agree that it is important to move forward and that the past serves as a guide for planning the future.

Once students have returned to their seats, I display an image of the Sankofa symbol via a projector or SMART Board. I ask students to work with a partner to take an "inquiry stance" for the image. In one minute, each partnership makes a list of as many questions as possible about the image. We then go around the room and have each partnership ask a question until all questions have been shared or three minutes are up. Students might ask: What is the bird holding in its mouth? Why is the bird's head turned backwards? No analysis is allowed at this time — only questions. The objective of the inquiry activity is for students to invite each other's analysis through their own questions.

At this point, I ask if anyone would like to decode the image and explain their reasoning by referencing details of the image. Then I introduce the concept of Sankofa and share the definition. I remind students that we've been looking at ways in which writers create utopias and imagine liberatory futures through poetry, and that today we are going to read two poems that position themselves toward the future while incorporating the past. I provide students with copies of the poems and, if possible, I project the poems on a SMART Board or with a projector.

As a class, we read the beginning of "dear white america" by Danez Smith:

dear white america
Danez Smith

dear white america

i've left Earth in search of darker planets, a solar system revolving too near a black hole. i've left in search of a new God. i do not trust the God you have given us. my grandmother's hallelujah is only outdone by the fear she nurses every time the blood-fat summer swallows another child who used to sing in the choir. take your God back. though his songs are beautiful, his miracles are inconsistent. i want the fate of Lazarus for Renisha, want Chucky, Bo, Meech, Trayvon, Sean & Jonylah risen three days after their entombing, their ghost re-gifted flesh & blood, their flesh & blood re-gifted their children. i've left Earth, i am equal parts sick of your *go back to Africa* & *i just don't see race.* neither did the poplar tree. we did not build your boats (though we did leave a trail of kin to guide us home). we did not build your prisons (though we did & we fill them too). we did not ask to be part of your America (though are we not America? her joints brittle & dragging a ripped gown through Oakland?). i can't stand your ground. i'm sick of calling your recklessness the law. each night, i count my brothers. & in the morning, when some do not survive to be counted, i count the holes they leave. i reach for black folks & touch only air. your master magic trick, America. now he's breathing, now he don't. abra-cadaver. white bread voodoo. sorcery you claim not to practice, hand my cousin a pistol to do your work. i tried, white people. i tried to love you, but you spent my brother's funeral making plans for brunch, talking too loud next to his bones. you took one look at the river, plump with the body of boy after girl after sweet boi & ask *why does it always have to be about race?* because you made it that way! because you put an asterisk on my sister's gorgeous face! call her pretty (for a black girl)! because black girls go missing without so much as a whisper of where?! because there are no amber alerts for amber-skinned girls! because Jordan boomed. because Emmett whistled. because Huey P. spoke. because Martin preached. because black boys can always be too loud to live. because it's taken my papa's & my grandma's time, my father's time, my mother's time, my aunt's time, my uncle's time, my brother's & my sister's time . . . how much time do you want for your progress? i've left Earth to find a place where my kin can be safe, where black people ain't but people the same color as the good, wet earth, until that means something, until then i bid you well, i bid you war, i bid you our lives to gamble with no more. i've left Earth & i am touching everything you beg your telescopes to show you. i'm giving the stars their right names. & this life, this new story & history you cannot steal or sell or cast overboard or hang or beat or drown or own or redline or shackle or silence or cheat or choke or cover up or jail or shoot or jail or shoot or jail or shoot or ruin

this, if only this one, is ours.

The first time we read the poem together, I interrupt them after the first five sentences and ask the class to collaboratively answer a few questions that ground students for the small group discussions that follow. I might ask: *What's happening in the poem so far? To whom might the pronouns refer? Who are the people named? What do the allusions reference? Is there any evidence of the Sankofa principle?*

I find that it's important to pause the conversation while the student excitement and desire to discuss is still high so that the meat of the discussion can take place in the small groups.

To transition to the second poem, I ask students to name other ways in which a poet can honor the past in addition to paying tribute to people who have been treated with injustice in the United

States. After two or three students share ideas and we've identified honoring our family and ancestors as another way to honor the past, we read the beginning of "big bang theory" by t'ai freedom ford.

big bang theory
for my granny,
Lillie Mae Ford
t'ai freedom ford

big bang theory
>*for my granny, Lillie Mae Ford*

in theory, she big bang.
her brown round lump of a body
stardusting half dozen babies into being
and giving God all the glory.

first Junior, who sprang to 6'4" like his daddy
ate up everything including the cardboard
pickled his tongue in sips of thunderbird
till shriveled liver polka-dotted his hands and lips pink.

Sista came next, wearing Ethel like storm cloud
and hex, shamed her into Angelina, meaning:
messenger of God but she big
and unpretty as a heathen.

Doris Yvonne got all the pretty and the skinny
and the crazy, so folks couldn't covet.
at 6, she saw colors fuzzed round people
thought everybody had this rainbow vision.

then in 1952, my mama brown-nosed herself
here. granny named her Amber, a quiet, too-dark
punk of a girl, ass-whippings all the way home
from school. married her fool-self off at 14.

Wayne came out in handcuffs. did not
pass go. went straight to jail. met
Muhammad and became Ramel
became crackhead became ghost.

Pamela named me. cute as she wanna be
spoiled with religion, granny's baby
spent half her life in the church testifying
to chicken wings, getting her holyghost on.

granny big bang. sequined hat
gangster. kicked Otis senior out
for mucking up her doilies with
engine grease. grandbabies everywhere.

fat as pork rinds and hungry as slaves.
she banged pots til they bled gravy,
banged her big body to the floor
in stroke. invented: serious as a heart attack.

she buried all the men with Jesus
on her breath. and when her big-boned
self big-banged to dust, we didn't call
it death. we called it magic.

After we read the first three stanzas together, we collaboratively answer a few questions to ground students for their small group discussion. I might ask: *What's happening in the poem so far? To whom might the pronouns refer? Who are the people who are named? Do you notice any evidence of the Sankofa principle?*

In my tenth-grade class, I allow students to choose which poem they want to read and discuss in a small group. For example, if fifteen students are interested in reading "big bang theory," I divide them into three groups of five. However, depending on the students' level of experience in collaborating as self-directed groups, I also might pre-assign groups of four or five students to each of the poems. (Depending on students' comfort and experience with analyzing poems, one might choose to look at and discuss the poems as a class instead of having the students work in small groups.)

Once students are grouped, I give them the task. First, identify two students who will read the entire poem aloud to the group. Then, invite each group member share their favorite line.

Finally, prepare to present the answers to the following questions to the rest of the class:

1. What do you think this poem is mostly about?

2. Where is there evidence of the Sankofa principle? Provide one example of how this poem envisions a liberatory future while "looking back."

3. What are the "poem ingredients" someone could follow to write their own poem?

Part Two: Writing in Response

If the students are comfortable working independently, I give the class a fifteen-minute reading period to read both poems to themselves. Otherwise, I would ask one or two students to read the poems aloud to the class. Next, we review the "poem ingredients" that were generated by students during the first part of the lesson, and I ask each student to finalize their decision about which poem they'd like to write after.

My tenth-grade students came up with the following ingredients:

If you want to write a poem inspired by "dear white america"
by Danez Smith:

- Write about leaving earth to find a better place (i.e. where there is no racism, sexism, etc.).
- Use repetition ("I have left earth…").
- Use similes and metaphors to make comparisons.
- Use stories from the past (American history or other histories).

If you want to write a poem inspired by "big bang theory" by
t'ai freedom ford:

- Choose one person that came before you in your family (e.g., grandparent, aunt).

- Compare the person to the "big bang" or choose a different scientific phenomenon or theory.
- Write whatever you know about that person or make stuff up.
- Include other family members related to that person.
- Write four-line stanzas.
- Create one stanza about each person.
- Use imagery and descriptive language.

The prompts provide students with differentiated entry points for honoring the past in their poems. Students who don't want to bring in history and current events can write about family. After students write, we hold a class reading in which every student reads a draft of their own poem.

The Sankofa principle has become a roadmap for my thinking about curriculum. Students often complain that their history classes are irrelevant. But I want students to see that they are history. I want students to make the connection between what they've inherited and the future that is theirs to create; to honor their ancestors and teachers while being free to dream the futures they deserve. The poems that the students write during this unit invite them to see their own lives and experiences as authentic and valid contributions to both literature and history. I continue to hold Khalilah's admonishment near my heart and ensure there is joy in the curriculum. While struggle is an important part of the two poems we explore in this lesson, both honor those who have come before as well as the joyful possibility of what may follow.

History and All Its Bright Particulars

Letter Writing and Poetry

by Tina Cane

As any teacher knows, it's not uncommon to walk into a US classroom and find students who have never read or written a poem. Some children arrive in kindergarten never having held a book. Still, almost all have composed a note or a letter. These dispatches may have been emails or emoji-heavy texts, but they were communiqués all the same. No matter which century we live in, interpersonal correspondence will always find a form. People need and want to say things to each other. Whatever else changes, that impulse will always remain.

As a visiting poet, I have always particularly loved working in history classes or during a social studies block. Teaching the work of poets in this context helps students to make connections, and to see the human story in history. Poetry also helps them to understand distant events as experienced by individuals, and to see those experiences through the creative lens.

During my initial visit to a history class, I frequently begin with a discussion about letter writing and our experiences of writing to other people, how forms have changed over time, and the impact of those changes. As the students wonder why there's a poet teaching in their history course, I steer the conversation towards the nature of historical documents and sources. I ask the class to imagine stumbling upon a bundle of letters tied with string, or a flash drive flush with emails. We usually agree that such a find would be a treasure trove of information — not just in regard to content, but also about the lives of the correspondents. Even the most mundane accounts of a person's day contain details that paint a portrait of an era. I encourage students to see their own lives as history in the making. History = life + time, I tell them.

In our discussion, we might think about what a letter inked in cursive and put on a ship reveals about a culture's relationship with time. We might consider how a hastily-written text — rife with acronyms — holds clues to the way we live today.

And then we shift to literature.

Many students, and even teachers, do not consider literature as historical document. Still, it's impossible to read Hawthorne or Hardy, Virginia Woolf or Pablo Neruda — or really any writer — without understanding this writer as a product of his or her era.

Allen Ginsberg's poem "America" leaps to mind, as he fixes his experience to a date and place in time:

> America I've given you all and now I'm nothing.
> America two dollars and twentyseven cents January 17, 1956.

Such a scant pair of lines, but rich with information on emerging style and form, and the poet-citizen's disillusionment with a relationship gone wrong. Even science fiction and fantasy — often devoid of contemporary detail or historic allusion — can provide insight into a writer's time by virtue of vision, genre, and motif. Think *Animal Farm*.

Once students are attuned to the idea that literature and history don't belong in separate boxes — and should probably be taught in tandem — we turn to writing. And we write letters — letters to someone we truly care about, so they will be good. Letters that we would be proud to have found a hundred years from now.

And, of course, we read William Carlos Williams' "This is Just to Say," because it was a note before it was a poem.

This Is Just to Say

I have eaten
the plums
that were in
the icebox

and which
you were probably
saving
for breakfast

Forgive me
they were delicious

This Is Just to Say
William Carlos Williams

so sweet

and so cold

The poem's spare form and conversational tone connote an important shift in poetry — one that reflects cultural and literary changes that were underway after World War I. While the premise of the poem is timeless, the word *icebox* locates it in an era when a fridge was, quite literally, a box with a hunk of ice in it. Students appreciate how that one word holds clues to others in the poem.

It usually takes a one-hour visit to lay the groundwork, introduce Williams' poem, and write a letter. When we get to letter writing, we might start with the phrase "this is just to say." We might choose to say something breezy and light, or write about a matter of grave importance.

Once we've shared some letters, we see about turning them into poems. This can happen during the second session, and there are many approaches to doing this. I usually ask students to circle the juiciest words, images, or phrases. After observing how the circled words often distill the letter's message, we move to rearranging the words on a fresh page. We use its open space to try out short lines like Williams, and to explore which kinds of choices impact the poem with regard to content.

Here is where I emphasize my definition of a poem as "words arranged in space that the poet says is a poem." Since poetry is a most flexible form, I stress the importance of *intention*. The poem becomes a poem because it is no longer intended to be a letter. "Can anything be a poem, then?" someone always calls out. "Yes!" someone else always responds, "If you say so!"

Once the students have produced an original poem, they are ready for "Today" by Frank O'Hara:

Today
Frank O'Hara

Today

Oh! kangaroos, sequins, chocolate sodas!
You really are beautiful! Pearls,

harmonicas, jujubes, aspirins! all
the stuff they've always talked about

still makes a poem a surprise!
These things are with us every day
even on beachheads and biers. They
do have meaning. They're strong as rocks.

"Today" is exuberant, refreshing, and mystifying to young readers. Written in 1950, its title resides beyond the constraints of time, while its jaunty catalogue has acquired a vintage patina:

… kangaroos, sequins, chocolate sodas! …
Pearls, / harmonicas, jujubes, aspirins!

The list itself embodies William Carlos Williams' assertion: "No idea / but in things." We see how punctuation creates energy and discover how a small poem can capture a whole philosophy of poetry: "…all / the stuff they've always talked about… These things are with us every day… They / do have meaning." The poem's breezy style belies its crucial message about poetics. It's not a letter, but it's still telling us something. Or as one student remarked, "Actually, it's kind of a letter, too."

"Dear David" by Matthew Burgess is a wonderful way to round out these sessions, for as Burgess says, "This poem is a transcript of a recent Sunday, a note written and sent to its recipient on the spot."

Dear David

This morning I looked
for your book online
and almost bought it
from the evil giant

Dear David
Matthew Burgess

but balked. Instead
I wrote a poem in bed
about a faux-leopard
jacket while drinking
coffee from a Bette
Midler mug. Marcel
says when he catches
himself self-censoring
he knows to add it
anyway. Anyway
I scrambled eggs
before rearranging
my book shelves,
extracting the ones
I can live without.
Those I put in a box
for prisoners (who
want dictionaries
and classic fiction,
the website says)
and later the buyer
in Red Hook took
a towering stack
for a seventeen buck
credit. I skimmed
the spines and there
you were! Like new!
On the cover in blue
pants, a violet plaid
shirt, surrounded by
bright particulars!

So, here we have a letter transposed into a poem by way
of *intention*. Chock full of the light, "bright particulars" O'Hara
proclaimed to be "strong as rocks," it's a poem anchored in the
present day, yet alive with the eternal nature of serendipity. The
"evil giant" of Amazon is out-favored by the kinder, gentler kitsch

of *faux-leopard* and a *Bette Midler mug*. At once about process, ("Marcel / says when he catches / himself self-censoring / he knows to add it / anyway..."), "Dear David" also resists process ("I wrote a poem in bed") and by doing so, keeps itself open for discovery: "there / you were! Like new!" The beauty of the poem is that it keeps us open, too. Poems, like history, are not created in a vacuum. They are both products of chance, confluence, and revision.

Deft and delightful, Burgess' poem brings us full circle. By now, students are usually comfortable enough to try writing letters that sound like letters, but look like poems, and are loaded with "bright particulars." And so we do that. And we imagine a future person finding our work, bundled and tied with string à la Emily Dickinson. What would they think? What would they glean? What "evil giant" will they be contending with a hundred years from now?

I taught these poems a couple of years ago in a world history course at a small charter high school in Rhode Island for pregnant and parenting teenagers, and for students in special circumstances — such as refugees or those living in group homes. The school provides a robust support network to increase students' chances of being college-bound. Many students are English language learners and most are performing below grade level. I spent three years working with students at the school, and my time there had an important impact on me as a teacher, a poet, and a parent. On an audio recording of my Writers in the Schools, RI program, produced by Atticus Allen, you can hear our class in action, as well as students reading the poems included here.

It's worth adding that although Enrique was new to English when he wrote his poems, he made amazing breakthroughs. The force of Enrique's love for his daughter propelled him to find the words. It also compelled him to instinctively write a heart-shaped concrete poem, even though he had never encountered one before.

"Birth" by Rhakiera is the only poem this student wrote during the entire semester. She was struggling on many fronts, and I sat with her as she pieced together her notes and built the poem. When it came time to record audio in our makeshift studio — the tiny nurse's office — Rhakiera flatly refused. She finally agreed when I offered to coach her through the recording.

When we played the finished audio piece, Enrique wasn't in school because he had to work that day. Christopher locked himself in the bathroom because he was so self-conscious about hearing his poem. Rhakiera, smiling faintly, kept shaking her head. "That's my voice," she said. "Damn."

Birth

Young Asian and Caucasian doctors
dim lights, grandma cheering
Asian doctor clapping
I was breathing heavy & pushing
Za'riyah out
Za'riyah's coming slowly
pulling and tugging,
Za'riyah crying Za'riyah
very pale, no eyebrows
Za'riyah 7 lbs. & 15 oz., 21 inches long
Hazel eyes open wide, long sandy hair
12 hours later Za'riyah gets bathed
smells like *Johnson & Johnson* lotion
We fall asleep for the whole night

Rhakeira W.

This is Just to Say

<pre>
                    Day   light
                windows,   sadness,
            madness, happi   ness, shadows
        light is stronger and it lights the d-
        arkness. Fear, strength, weaknesss, tear-
        s, love, but love surpasses everything.
            Growing, Time, busy, spoon, plate, f-
                ood, floor, carpet, you're there
                    and you're always in my h-
                    eart when i am absen-
                        t. Daddy,daught-
                            er, Baby m-
                                y fami
                                ly.
</pre>

Enrique L.

Just Stick to You

Trying to graduate is like
Running forever
You feel like
Forrest Gump
A kid they said could not walk or run
But he kept trying and trying
And eventually he did it
You need to break out of them braces
Like he did

Life is moving
Slow as molasses
Then picks up faster than a roadrunner
Running through the desert
You know you want to be
Like a Rothschild

You need an education to get that money

Everyone wants to be like Drake

But
They put in no work
Just stick to you
And
Life will be filled with
Money, cars, clothes,
Whatever your heart desires
But you got to watch out
With that money
There are always snakes in the grass
Money has the power to
Change people
Especially you

Sincerely,

Your Conscience

Christopher M.

Wish You Were Here!
Using Postcards to Inspire Poetry

by Bianca Stone

Over the years I have been collecting postcards, mostly found, some received, and, happily, a good many inherited ones from poets including Ruth Stone, Sharon Olds, and James Tate. I love both the random and specific nature of postcards. Here you may find a tiny scene photographed of some obscure tourism site, but also great art, downsized; literary figures like flash cards; obscene puns and catchy idioms from beach scenes; and lots of geographical information you never cared to know. Postcards are the perfect portable ekphrastic muse.

The New York School poets are a great example of writers who interact with objects such as the postcard. I'm thinking of Frank O'Hara's *Lunch Poems*, and John Ashbery, who made wonderful collages from postcards, which absolutely mirror his methods in poems. James Schuyler and artist and poet Joe Brainard also often employed postcards in their poetry and art, respectively.

Wallace Stevens' "A Postcard from the Volcano" is an address from the natural beyond: "Children picking up our bones / Will never know that these were once / As quick as foxes on the hill." Steve Kistulentz's "Postcard from a Place I Have Never Been" plays with movement, alternate reality of travel, and the disconnect of personality: "I play a slightly amplified / version of myself, with one line: *Wish you were here*." Sjohnna McCray's "Postcard: Turning Stations" is a stark snapshot of America, 1972, ghosting back to us in the present, illuminating just enough to send chills. It seems sometimes that poems themselves are textual postcards: place, painting, snapshot, sent-out glimpses of a something someone has witnessed.

Ruth Stone's "Imprint of the Stereoscopic Cards" shows the frightening fascination of more antiquated postcards used for world-news purposes. Her poem "For a Post Card of My Mother at the Beach" is another vivid example that could be included as a lead-in to the following lesson.

For a Post Card of My Mother at the Beach
Ruth Stone

For a Post Card of My Mother at the Beach

My oyster weeps the pearls of denouement.
Oh dolorous beach where dead white ladies dance

In spanking striped beach garments, I may weep
And click my shells for pearls of indiscretion,
My oyster is gray raw.
Into the surf plunges a striped procession.

Ladies, ladies, lifting your dry old toes,
How sagging are those stripes, how sad it goes.
Into the rock rimmed pools I cast my tears,
Pearls for your sandy steps,
Sand for your churly lips,
The meanest pearls, and wasted as ocean weirs.

What Stone does well in this poem is meld her own life into the images of the postcard. (It is unlikely that this is actually an image of her mother.) She mingles realities by transferring into the scene via oyster and pearl. We can imagine that the original image was just of old-fashioned women bathing. From there, so much comes to the witness, the speaker. There is this element of sending a letter to the dead in a postcard poem; cards are elegies, sent from here and from beyond. But the spark of inspiration is key in this ekphrastic — and elegiac — exercise.

How can we enter into an image and find a spark for our own creation? We need not be beholden to the image throughout our poem; rather we find something that engages our brain in a new way, that encourages a different vocabulary, visually and lyrically.

How it works: The first part of this prompt is coming up with captions for postcards, which can bring new meaning to images, exploring our power with words. The second part is taking that line further, playing off the image of the card, going deeper with one image in particular. A bonus of the prompt is in the nature of letter writing; think of this as a love letter or gift to someone else. So, the writer becomes inspired by the image of the card, the context of that image, as well as the awareness of communication with another.

To prepare, bring as many postcards as people doing the prompt, or more. If there is just one person, then have four or five cards to work with. Here are the instructions that I give to my students.

1. Write a caption or one-line poem for each card.

2. After you've written one caption, pass your card to the right. Continue until you get your first card back.

3. Share with one another the different captions, and notice how they change your perception of the image on the card. What new meanings do we perceive, now that the picture has this caption?

4. Write a poem beginning with one of the lines.

5. Share out loud!

   Alternatives:

   - Write a poem on the back of each postcard in the form of a letter to someone.
   - Use a huge stack of cards, and time yourself. You have only ten minutes to write as many captions as you can.
   - Write a collage poem using all your captions.

Perhaps what strikes me about postcards — as a writer, artist, and poetry comics maker — is that they are a vehicle by which, universally, people share words and pictures with one another. Like published poetry, they go off into the world to be read (maybe by the mailperson), the text interpreted and image absorbed, the gift given with no requirement of response beyond the act of receiving. What I've found in using this exercise with students is sometimes it can feel difficult at first to come up with a "caption" for the card. But I think that difficulty gets at the point of this: find a flow that allows for language to come without overthinking meaning. It enables you to get in touch with your immediate, visceral reaction to a picture, which is ekphrastic practice, something the Greeks took very seriously as a rhetorical device, a vital resource in language as a means of communication that might elicit an emotional response.

Really, the postcard is easy access to visual art. It is words and pictures coming together. It is a size constraint. A 5×7 tool of inspiration. It's also a delightful practice to mail postcards with poems on the back to your colleagues and to amass a collection of them. (The poet Emily Pettit has been sending them to me for years and it is one of the highlights of checking my mailbox!) Postcards are a product of our culture and our very specific eras. They say something about civilization. And, they're very cheap to buy.

Here is an example from one of my students writing a poem inspired from this desert postcard. It is an almost clichéd image of a cactus but all her vivid and specific associations bloom from that iconic image, creating a fresh narrative poem. I encourage my students to respond visually if they feel compelled as well. Here, she has taken the associations brought forth from the exercise and created a new image. Ekphrastic prompts need not produce only text, and I think it's incredible to allow yourself ample room to explore different creative responses and how far you might take something.

Urban Legend

A woman takes a cactus home, it pulses open on her coffee table,
and spiders fill the house. She, my wild Aunt Julie, a legend, collected
the story out west where she took up boyfriends and left them behind,
brought me a terracotta pot still ringing with the Eagles songs
she blasted in her jeep. I'd have followed her through the desert
even when she said it was her house, her cactus, and at least one in every
    ten cacti
bristles with tarantulas. In my head, I saw them crouching in the
    dusty dark
as lightning walked toward them, as shaggy with light as their feathery
    brains.
The sky, violet, hung low and close as love, crackled their hairs, my
    hairline.
My saguaro ribs ached for desert. She seemed a woman built of thrill.

But in her story, she could never say what happened after,
after the man from animal control told her to run from the house,
a storm of spiders looming. And now, we hardly talk.
She lives alone by the lake, a tough woman building a tight house
from scratch. What if I am like her, as I had always hoped?
Hard, alone, aching in my exoskeleton, a knot of lightning
on my tongue, and irreparably soft. Whatever's coming,
I want to bear it, to hear it as song, open my fists to the rain,
even if all the stories I know are fiction and my heroes, tired.

In dreams, I return to our landscapes, our pine, our birches,
where I walked with her in the woods to collect spring water.
I sleep on a mountain that shifts underneath, warm with pine boughs
and bodies. From this view, each step is new, as though
lightning strikes bolt each moment open one flash at a time.
I don't care that she lied. She taught me this thrill.

Meg Reynolds

A WOMAN TAKES A CACTUS HOME, IT PULSES ON HER COFFEE TABLE, THEN SPIDERS FILL THE HOUSE. MY WILD AUNT JULIE, A LEGEND, COLLECTED THE STORY OUT WEST WHERE SHE TOOK UP BOYFRIENDS AND LEFT THEM BEHIND, BROUGHT ME BACK TERRACOTTA POTS STILL HUMMING WITH THE EAGLES SONGS SHE BLASTED IN HER JEEP. I'D HAVE FOLLOWED HER THROUGH THE DESERT EVEN AFTER SHE SAID IT WAS HER HOUSE, HER CACTUS, AND THAT ONE IN TEN CACTI BRISTLES WITH TARANTULAS. IN MY HEAD, I SAW THEM CROUCHING IN THE DUSTY DARK AS LIGHTNING WALKED TOWARD THEM AS SHAGGY WITH LIGHT AS THEIR FEATHERY BRAINS. THE SKY, VIOLET, HUNG LOW AND CLOSE AS LOVE, CRACKLED THEIR HAIRS, MY HAIRLINE. MY SAGUARO RIBS ACHED FOR DESERT. SHE SEEMED A WOMAN BUILT OF THRILL. BUT IN HER STORY, SHE COULD NEVER SAY WHAT HAPPENED AFTER, AFTER THE MAN FROM ANIMAL CONTROL TOLD HER TO RUN FROM THE HOUSE, A STORM OF SPIDERS COMING. WE HARDLY TALK THESE DAYS SHE LIVES ALONE BY THE LAKE, A TOUGH LADY BUILDING A TIGHT HOUSE FROM SCRATCH. WHAT IF I AM LIKE HER, AS I'D ALWAYS HOPED? HARDENING ALONE, ACHING IN MY EXOSKELETON, A KNOT OF LIGHTNING ON MY TONGUE, AND, AT MY MIDDLE, IRREPARABLY SOFT? WHATEVER'S COMING, I WANT TO BEAR IT, HEAR IT AS A SONG, OPEN MY FISTS TO THE RAIN, EVEN IF EVERY STORY I KNOW IS FICTION, AND MY HEROES, TIRED. IN DREAMS, I RETURN TO OUR LANDSCAPES, OUR PINE AND BIRCHES WHERE I ONCE WALKED WITH HER TO TELL STORIES AND COLLECT SPRING WATER. THERE, I SLEEP HALF WAY UP A MOUNTAIN THAT SHIFTS UNDERNEATH, WARM WITH BOUGHS AND BEASTS. IT'S THE MOUNTAIN'S SHOULDER OR HER SHOULDER. FROM THIS VIEW EACH STEP IS NEW AS THOUGH LIGHTNING BOLTS MOMENTS OPEN ONE AT A TIME. I DON'T CARE THAT SHE LIED. I CLIMB, OPEN TO THE THRILL SHE TAUGHT ME

DAY 287

Beatbox and Other Experiments

A List of Poetry Prompts

by Todd Colby

During my many years of teaching poetry-writing workshops to young and old alike, I've used the following prompts with terrific results. They invite participants to tell stories about their lives through minute particulars, and they lead to both personal discoveries and a communal recognition of our quirky similarities. The idea of authorship for a lot of poets, whether they are young or old, is often a barricade to simply having fun while writing poetry. Leveling the playing field with prompts invites everyone to participate — an important step in loosening the grip of trepidation and self-consciousness and letting the ideas flow freely with joy!

Beatbox Writing Prompt: Try to remember the first device on which you listened to music. Now, describe the device as vividly as possible, making note of the brand, the color, the physical attributes, the weight, the feel of it, and any peculiarities about it. Feel free to make a sketch of the device to enhance your memory of it. Second, make a list of the names of the bands, musicians, composers, or orchestras that you played through that device. Was the music on a cassette, a vinyl LP, a CD, or an MP3? Once the list is made, go back and try to conjure up details, emotions, thoughts, and impressions of each of the names on the list. Where did you listen to music on the device? Did you listen to a sad song while breaking up with someone? While mad at your parents? While confused about something at school? Which lyrics do you still remember? Which lyrics moved you then, but embarrass you now? If your listening device had been equipped with a camera, what is something it would have recorded you doing while listening to a favorite song? Let the list you assemble serve as your guide while the memories unfold. Remember to be fearless and affectionate with your past musical self.

Inventory Prompt: Sit in a comfortable chair and write down, as precisely, vividly, and patiently as possible, everything within your immediate field of vision. Feel free to add any sounds you hear, conversations you overhear, smells you detect, and any memories these things conjure up. Remember, every single detail is essential, and nothing is inconsequential.

Overheard Poem Prompt: Sit in a public space where a lot of people are talking. A lunchroom is a perfect place to write this poem. Pretend you are a spy, listening to people talking around you without letting them know you're listening. Write down everything you can hear the people around you saying, even things you *think* you hear.

Subway or Bus Poem Prompt: Find a seat on a subway car or in a bus. Write a short poem between every stop on the subway or bus (starting when the doors close and stopping only when they open). Don't stop to think about what you are writing; simply observe, listen, daydream, and write. Make lists, write down what people are saying or doing. What shoes are people wearing? Is anyone wearing an interesting hat? The options are endless! Remember, only write while the train or bus is motion.

Interview Poem Prompt: Make a list of ten questions. Interview a friend for five minutes while writing down the answers. Make a poem or prose piece from the notes. Example conversation starters: When was the last time you cried? In one sentence, describe the plot of the last movie you saw. Name three cities you've been to and describe each one in one sentence. Describe the last meal you had, using brand names if applicable.

Bad Poem Prompt: Write the worst poem you possibly can. Use every bad cliché as you write your poem. Go to Google Translate and translate the poem into at least five different languages and then back into English. Don't edit the results. There's your poem.

Subtraction Poem Prompt: See if you can write a poem without using any nouns or adjectives, adverbs or gerunds, or any variation you choose, while describing a sunset, yourself in the mirror, or a beautiful landscape. Try to use the constraints to your advantage. Invent your own constraints and watch what happens when you sit down to write a poem.

Factory Poem Prompt (based on Exquisite Corpse): Sit around a table with a group of people (the more the merrier!). Everyone should have a blank sheet of paper. Ask everyone to write a title, and then pass the page to your neighbor on your left. Write the first line under the title. Pass to your left. And so on until the piece of paper with your title comes back to you. Don't stop to read the title or the writing before yours. For extra credit: Try writing a Factory Poem with distractions. Ask someone not participating in the Factory Poem to read aloud, sing, tell a story, or play the radio while everyone is writing their Factory Poem. Some of the distractions might end up in the poem.

Epistolary Poem Prompt: Write a letter to the editor about the history of your favorite shirt. Be as specific as possible. Where did you buy the shirt? What important events have happened to you while wearing the shirt? Where have you travelled while wearing the shirt?

Soothing Poem Prompt: Write the world's most soothing poem. Try to write a poem that soothes whoever reads it. What are words or images that are soothing to you? What sounds or smells do you find relaxing? How do you fit those things into a poem? Try to write a poem that puts whoever reads it into a delightful, relaxed state of mind.

Alien Voice-to-Text Prompt: Use the voice-to-text feature on a smartphone as you walk to a destination. As you dictate into your phone, imagine you are transmitting messages to a civilization in another galaxy that has no idea what is going on here on Earth. What do you think the person who has never been here would like to know about? Try to be as clear and specific as possible. For extra fun, try to include the inevitable mistakes the voice-to-text feature on your smartphone makes as you dictate into it.

Word Poem Prompt: If you're working alone, make a list of ten favorite words. Use those words in the same order in a poem, letting each word lead you through the poem. Try to make each word fit into the poem so it flows. If you're working in a group, have everyone pick ten words as a group, then have the entire group write their own poems using the same ten words the group chose.

Wild Thing

Love Poems and Self-Portraits Inspired by Donika Kelly's *Bestiary*

by Melissa Febos

As a memoirist and essayist, I teach primarily creative nonfiction courses. Perhaps we can all agree that among creative writing students, those drawn to creative nonfiction tend to be comfortable, or at least interested, in a direct confrontation of their own most painful and confounding life experiences. That is, I can tell a class of aspiring memoirists to take out their notebooks and, write a scene of personal humiliation from your adolescence, and they will all begin furiously scribbling. After the exercise, when I ask who wants to share their work, their arms, however tentative, wave like reeds.

Recently I taught my first undergrad poetry class. *Take out your notebooks*, I said, and they did. *Write a sensory description of a personal humiliation from your adolescence*, I said. Fifteen pairs of eyes blinked up at me. Cheeks reddened. Breath quickened. Aspiring poets, it turns out, seem less inclined to this sort of direct confrontation with the past.

They delighted, however, at exploring a poem's multiple interpretations. Glimpsing that painful memory from behind the cracked door of an image or shifting beneath the cloak of metaphor gave them the same giddy triumph that direct exposure did my memoirists. They particularly loved the work of Donika Kelly in her debut collection, *Bestiary*. Kelly's work is profoundly personal, but often uses figures from mythology and the natural world to approach subjects of heartache, loneliness, longing, and trauma.

Two sequences in the collection particularly spoke to my students. One included the poems "Love Poem: Centaur," "Love Poem: Mermaid," and "Love Poem: Satyr." The other, "Self-Portrait as a Door" and "Self-Portrait as a Block of Ice." The idea that they could use the mythology of a beast or the persona of an object, and express their own sorrows and joys through those aspects and voices, set their pens scribbling.

Love Poem: Mermaid

Do you ever look into a mirror,
which is also an ocean heavy with sun?

Love Poem: Mermaid
Donika Kelly

Do you ever pull your hair,
wet, over your shoulders to dry

as you sit and sing for another's
death? Love, I am made

for calling: bare breast, smooth tail,
the perfect balance of scales.

I have claimed this rock,
which is also your heart,

which is also a shell I hold
to my ear to hear what is right

in front of me. I am a witness
to the sea and the sun, to your body

lashed to the mast. O that my voice
were a knife, that a knife could change

anything, that there was nothing
between us but salt and breath.

**Self-Portrait
as a Door**
Donika Kelly

Self-Portrait as a Door

All the birds die of blunt-force trauma —
of barn of wire of *YIELD* or *SLOW
CHILDREN AT PLAY.* You are a sign
are a plank are a raft are a felled oak.
You are a handle are a turn are a bit
of brass lovingly polished.
What birds what bugs what soft
hand come knocking. What echo
what empty what room in need
of a picture a mirror a bit of paint
on the wall. There is a hooked rug.

There is a hand hard as you are hard
pounding the door. There is the doormat
owl eye patched by a boot by a body
with a tree for a hand. What roosts
what burrows what scrambles
at the pound. There is a you
on the other side, cold and white
as the room, in need of a window
or an eye. There is your hand
on the door which is now the door
pretending to be a thing that opens.

After reading the poems together, we brainstormed a list
of all the mythical beasts we could think of, from vampires
to unicorns to gryphons. Then, I asked each student to choose
a beast. We spent a few minutes researching our beasts, their
origins and characteristics. (Though I generally ban smartphone
usage in class, I find them to be useful for this kind of on-the-
spot fact gathering.) Finally, I gave the students a choice: love
poem or self-portrait. I asked them to incorporate some of
their research and to draw from their own personal experience
in some way. They were free to calibrate the poem's distance
from that experience according to their own comfort or
aesthetic preference.

This freedom suited them. Many used the first person
to inhabit the persona of their beast. Others stepped to the
side with the second-person point of view. Some stayed quite
close to the narrative of their beast, grafting familiar emotions
onto those stories, while others used the mythologies more
impressionistically. All of them counted these poems among
their strongest, and their most personal, at the semester's end.

Transformation

Then. It took you in the back alley,
the moon full of ravenous hunger,

silver streams of light
casts dark shadows on the
ground, on the face, on the teeth;
the blood, roses in a field
gleams brightly from the white,
straight edged bite that
stole your humanity.

Now. The panic, heat rising,
dark fur running down your arms;
your back arches, bones crack,
pain — as heavy as a train
moving full speed crashing into you —
seeps through your veins.
Hunger. The deep cave of
wonder disappears, the hunger
so strong it shreds your insides,
until you can find your next victim.
Inch by inch, you are changed.
In a lurching crouch, you spring.

The white of his eyes and teeth
glow like the moon, the stars scattering
the night sky — and before he could move,
you sink your nails into his chest,
the blood spilling out like a waterfall.
The power, the control, it's an addiction.
You thirst for the hunt, you desire their
blood to cover you, to soak in their
desperation and hear their cries.

His eyes widen, the teeth chatters,
the scream barely escapes his lips
and you've already sunk the claws,
the dirty nails of dread and despair,
into the guttering chest; the blood,
so much blood, spills out like a broken
vase, a waterfall of red crimson. His

last breath, his final gasp with humanity,
and thus opens a deadly gate.

Abigail L. Fenn (Monmouth University)

Lost and Found
Reading and Writing the Elegy

by Michael Morse

There isn't anything that makes grief better, and I think artists have to accommodate that fact, in their work…That said, I truly don't know how people survive grief without making something out of it…. And that is no small thing…it can provide you with a place to stand, a margin that can save your life.

Mark Doty

All lyric poems have the essence of elegy in their DNA: they still and distill particular moments in time and make keepsakes of consciousness that survive the moment of their making. Elegies, however, explicitly address loss and move towards consolation and transformation: their appeal lies in turning loss — or threats of loss — into artful presence. Ron Padgett notes that *elegy* comes from the Greek word *elegeia*, which translates to "song of mourning." While classical elegies often name a specific loss, lament it, and finally move towards consolation, an elegy, as Mark Strand and Eavan Boland note, "is not associated with any required pattern." They define it as a "shaping form," more akin to "an environment" rather than an expression with a strict formal pattern.

Ovid's *Metamorphoses* offers us two mythological narratives that tap the wellsprings of elegiac poetry: the respective tales of Apollo and Daphne, and Pan and Syrinx. In both, misbehaving male gods pursue females whom they covet. Only the females' cries to be transformed save them, as Daphne is given the form of the laurel tree, and Syrinx, marsh reeds. Apollo, distraught at his loss, finds some consolation in the laurel wreath that he fashions out of Daphne's leaves, while Pan sighs, and "the reeds in his hands, stirred by his own breath, / [give] forth a similar, low pitched complaint!" In both tales, objects from the natural world are altered and yield a consoling instrument. Nature transforms to artifice, and loss, consolation. And while it's clear that Apollo and Pan don't deserve *any* consolations given their aggressions, these tales — warts and all — can help us face what's problematic about the behavior that myths model while also revealing the roots of the western elegy.

Effective elegies refuse to be singularly idiosyncratic — they reach outside of a purely personal experience of loss and grieving to allow for shared public sentiment.

Here's a lovely example:

Little Elegy
Keith Althaus

Little Elegy

Even the stars wear out.
Their great engines fail.
The unapproachable roar
and heat subside.
And wind blows across
the hole in the sky
with a noise like a boy
playing on an empty bottle.
It is an owl, or a train.
You hear it underground.
Where the worms live
that can be cut in half
and start over
again and again.
Their heart must be
in two places at once, like mine.

I love this poem's understated eloquence and clear vertical track from the celestial down into earth. The simple-yet-deft earthworm analogy at poem's end yields a moving simultaneity of feeling that fills our best poetry — one heart in two different places. A modern elegy, it's grounded by a figure — a boy's breath over an empty bottle — that recalls the mythological wellsprings of western elegies found in Ovid's tales of Pan and Syrinx and Apollo and Daphne; both gods are left with natural materials (marsh reeds and laurel leaves) that they shape into consoling instruments (pipes that play music; a wreath that can be worn).

Here's another terrific contemporary elegy:

What the Living Do

Johnny, the kitchen sink has been clogged for days, some utensil probably
    fell down there.
And the Drano won't work but smells dangerous, and the crusty dishes have
    piled up

waiting for the plumber I still haven't called. This is the everyday we spoke of.
It's winter again: the sky's a deep headstrong blue, and the sunlight pours
    through

the open living room windows because the heat's on too high in here,
    and I can't turn it off.
For weeks now, driving, or dropping a bag of groceries in the street,
    the bag breaking,

I've been thinking: This is what the living do. And yesterday, hurrying along
    those
wobbly bricks in the Cambridge sidewalk, spilling my coffee down my wrist
    and sleeve,

I thought it again, and again later, when buying a hairbrush: This is it.
Parking. Slamming the car door shut in the cold. What you called *that*
    yearning.

What you finally gave up. We want the spring to come and the winter to pass.
    We want
whoever to call or not call, a letter, a kiss — we want more and more and
    then more of it.

But there are moments, walking, when I catch a glimpse of myself in the
    window glass,
say, the window of the corner video store, and I'm gripped by a cherishing
    so deep

for my own blowing hair, chapped face, and unbuttoned coat that I'm
    speechless:
I am living, I remember you.

Similarly matter-of-fact, Howe's poem features everyday iniquities — from bad plumbing to broken grocery bags — that accrue. And yet, with memory and desire comes a kind of salvation, a desperate love for what's present through the conciliatory memory of what's absent. At poem's end, remembering feels like a reward, consciousness and its bright prize of presence, where even what we've lost can accompany us.

The materiality of the world and the resonance of objects — whether laurel wreath or wind audible like breath over an empty bottle or one's face reflected in glass — can similarly evoke the departed and help us carry them forward. Such figuration can also help us to approach loss "from the side," via indirection, much as we choose not to look at the sun directly so that we might continue to see. What follows are two exercises that encourage a frank and direct look at loss while encouraging the fresh use of sensory perception and metaphor to evocatively figure loss and move forward. Before starting the exercises, you might have an informal conversation with students about what they've "lost." Please note that elegies need not involve "death," only loss, and any scenario when time and selves change (a graduation, autumn, the end of a year) can serve as elegiac inspiration.

The Apple Elegy

My favorite elegy exercise is one that my best friend and fellow poet Matthew Lippman developed, inspired by a poetic fragment originally from a Yiddish remedy book and reproduced in *Exiled in the World*, edited by Jerome Rothenberg and Harris Lenowitz.

> Slice an apple in three.
> Write a name on each slice & eat it.

I start by sharing Grace Schulman's poem "Apples," which, in addition to its references to Eve and Cézanne and ideas of beauty and exile, gives readers a rich catalogue of particular types of apples (e.g., Crimson King, Salome, Northern Spy). After some quizzical looks — *What does this have to do with elegy?* — and a brief discussion of the poem and its imagery, I ask students to brainstorm a list of any associations they can come up with involving the word *apple*: Adam and Eve, Johnny Appleseed, Snow White, iPhones, "an apple a day keeps the doctor away," and others will no doubt arise. Encourage kids to call out ideas and you'll soon have a board filled with a delightfully random list for later reference.

You'll then need a bunch of apples that you can cut into slices. As you section the apples, ask students to think about someone, some thing, or some place that they've "lost" — perhaps a beloved pet or family member. It might be a more figurative loss, say, a friend whom one hasn't seen in a decade since moving, or perhaps one's first home or town which has been left behind. Ask the students to picture the person, place, or thing in their mind's eye with as much sensory detail as possible. As they mull these thoughts, give each individual (provided they're not allergic or can't stand apples) a slice, a napkin, and a toothpick; then ask them to use the toothpick like a pen and "write" (more like punch, in staccato or pointillist fashion) the initials of their beloved person/pet/place into the skin of the apple. Then, with pencil and paper (or laptops) at the ready, they get to *eat* the apple, engaging with the sensory experience of *taste* as they *think* about their chosen subject. Do their tastes and memories correlate? What's sweet, pleasing, sour, or tart in either realm?

This mesh of memory and the palate's present moment offers a springboard from which they can now leap into writing. What's this experience like? Can they begin to capture on paper what it's like to ingest both apple and the memory of their subject? What, from the sensory experience of ingestion to the catalogue of the students' personal memories to the associations compiled on the board, can the students say about a specific being or place? Encourage your students to taste, reflect, and begin to write as they meditate on the experience of tasting both the apple itself and their loss. While any apple-related imagery and associations can serve as springboards into poems, it's also fine for students to veer away from apples towards whatever language they'd like to explore as they contemplate loss.

Here's an untitled "apple elegy" by former high-schooler Eddie:

Long summer days filled with nothing but joy
hiking through the wood with the curiosity of a child,
long nights of talking truth passing around liquid courage —
Loud so loud never wrong in his mind and more stubborn than an ox.
Small and thin almost a twin of my kin,
loyal and strong, first to throw a punch and ask forgiveness later,
unfairly taken from the ones he loved,
now partying with friends fallen in times of the past
and probably saying *hey, hurry up* and *move your ass.*
Us all like apples waiting to fall.
He fell sooner than the rest, almost plucked before his time to pass
but like all apples each has a seed
that will grow into a strong tree.
I sit under it thinking of good times past.

Eddie

I love how Eddie's imagination generates a landscape in which he can remember his lost friend and evokes a final tree image that suggests sitting with him even as he remembers him.

The Heirloom/Object Elegy

Another favorite exercise starts with students reading Eavan Boland's poem "The Black Lace Fan my Mother Gave Me," a poem where Boland writes about a fan that she still has: the first gift her father gave to her mother. Boland's poem begins with the silent object and magically recreates a distant evening and its dramatic context. The object becomes the springboard into elegy that rescues or even reinvents a past moment, bringing it alive in part by bringing in a striking metaphor at poem's end (the fan's opening likened to a bird's wing) that helps bridge past and present.

The Black Lace Fan My Mother Gave Me

It was the first gift he ever gave her,
buying it for five francs in the Galeries
in prewar Paris. It was stifling.
A starless drought made the nights stormy.

They stayed in the city for the summer.
They met in cafés. She was always early.
He was late. That evening he was later.
They wrapped the fan. He looked at his watch.

She looked down the Boulevard des Capucines.
She ordered more coffee. She stood up.
The streets were emptying. The heat was killing.
She thought the distance smelled of rain and lightning.

These are wild roses, appliqued on silk by hand,
darkly picked, stitched boldly, quickly.
The rest is tortoiseshell and has the reticent,
clear patience of its element. It is

a worn-out underwater bullion and it keeps,
even now, an inference of its violation.
The lace is overcast as if the weather
it opened for and offset had entered it.

The past is an empty café terrace.
An airless dusk before thunder. A man running.
And no way now to know what happened then —
none at all — unless, of course, you improvise:

the blackbird on this first sultry morning
in summer, finding buds, worms, fruit,
feels the heat. Suddenly she puts out her wing —
the whole, full, flirtatious span of it.

**The Black
Lace Fan
My Mother
Gave Me**
Eavan Boland

Having read and discussed the poem with the class, I ask the students to bring in some kind of inherited item: a small, portable, and backpack-durable object that has emotional significance for them—and the object has to be something that they received from, or associate with, someone else. First, we go around the room for a quick round of show & tell: each student presents an object— that pendant from a grandmother, that small knick-knack from an old friend who moved away—and discusses its resonance. Next, students take five minutes to write a prose description of their object, using the senses and descriptive adjectives and avoiding any narrative details, sticking only with the object's physical qualities. (Later on, they'll have a chance to engage freely with any associations and reflections that the objects and connections evoke.) I then ask students to circle the four most evocative adjectives from their descriptions and then list them, horizontally, across the top of a new page of notes, creating a column beneath each adjective. Beneath each adjective, they'll then generate three nouns that correspond only to the adjective atop the column (no connection to the objects is necessary). From each of these four columns, the students should circle the one noun that evokes the most wonder, and they'll save these four chosen nouns as a word bank for their future poem. Before setting the students loose to work on elegies using their chosen nouns and any other language they'd like to use concerning their object and the gift-giver/person-of-significance, we look at one more poem together.

Classic Ballroom Dances

Charles Simic

Classic Ballroom Dances

Grandmothers who wring the necks
Of chickens; old nuns
With names like Theresa, Marianne,
Who pull schoolboys by the ear;

The intricate steps of pickpockets
Working the crowd of the curious
At the scene of an accident; the slow shuffle
Of the evangelist with a sandwich-board;

The hesitation of the early-morning customer
Peeking through the window-grille
Of a pawnshop; the weave of a little kid
Who is walking to school with eyes closed;

And the ancient lovers, cheek to cheek,
On the dance floor of the Union Hall,
Where they also hold charity raffles
On rainy Monday nights of an eternal November.

Elegiac in tone if not a true elegy, Charles Simic's "Classic Ballroom Dances" generates a list of evocative figures — the careful steps of a pickpocket in a crowd, a little kid weaving his way to school with his eyes closed — that render daily actions on a busy street as *dances*. Just as Simic's catalogue of figures bolsters our vision, the storehouse of seemingly unrelated nouns offers additional avenues for poets to explore resonant connections and address presence and loss in both explicit and indirect fashion.

Finally, I give my students time to create freely, keeping the Simic and Boland poems close by as potential models of form and unfolding, and I urge them to give their poems a clear title that, as with Boland's poem, directly references the object and creates instant context for a reader.

Two recent students, Rebecca and Emily, brought in resonant objects that yielded sharp poems. Emily brought in a keychain that her late father had given her as a gift. Rebecca brought in a five-charm necklace that she received years back as a bat mitzvah gift. Below, you'll find the four adjectives each student chose from their preliminary, descriptive paragraphs and their corresponding list of nouns (I've put in boldface the nouns they chose to work with in their actual poems.), followed by the poem they created as their elegy.

*

Emily: electric (light bulb, love, **spark**); crisp (chip, **winter** edge); metallic (tool, **machine**, light); purple (violet, grape, **sunset**).

The Key Chain Clip My Father Gave Me

I learned from Taylor Swift that sparks fly.
As if those fleeting twinkles of light
possessed the wings of a firefly on a summer's eve;
so bright yet gone within the blink of an eye.
What were those tiny magical creatures
that I could not seem to catch,
dancing on the surface of the air
in a perfectly imperfect harmony?

I wondered why she said
"sparks fly when you smile,"
because I thought they only emerged from loud machines.
How could a human create something
that only metal could ignite?
I did not understand
why I could not conjure those sparks
that she sang about so longingly.

I yearned to capture this extraordinary light
like the happy children I used to watch on television,
who somehow found a way
to isolate fireflies in small jars
and transform their dreams into reality.
But in the winter time,
when the world was overcome by darkness,
I never understood how warmth could prevail
in such a cold and frigid world.

It was only on those warm nights,
when the sunset lit up the sky
as if God himself had formed a fire in the heavens,
that I felt hopeful that one day
sparks would fly when I smiled.
But those sunsets only lasted for so long
before they lost their color
and became black once again.

Now I know what Swift meant when she said that sparks fly.
Sometimes I still feel cold.
But now I carry a little spark with me wherever I go,
in the form of a key chain clip my father gave to me.
Some days I can see
those sparks that jump out from machines
glittering at the bottom of my backpack…
because the flame that was my father will never be extinguished.

Emily Power (11th grade)

Rebecca: Gold (corn, pirates, **necklace**); light blue (sky, **baby clothes**, water); purple (eggplant, **amethyst**, lilac); special (jewels, **love**, family).

My Identity on a Gold Chain

Whenever I reach my hands up to the sky
I feel like I am reaching for something
that will never come.

Why do my fingertips
feel like they will never be the same?
The baby clothes beneath my heavy heart
feel like a lifetime of unanswered questions.
Somewhere, somehow, I am a lost cause.
My anchor pulls me down
until I drift to the bottom of the ocean.

I will never know
if her eyes were filled with chocolate
or emerald, or amethyst.

This bottomless love
that will never reach an end
swallows me up

and I am lost in an ocean of stars.

The myths that hang around my neck
in golden shapes make me remember you.
Maybe if I wear this necklace forever
you will never leave me.

Rebecca Fields (11th grade)

Many thanks to Amy Rokicki and Margaret Phillips and Eddie, formerly of Provincetown High School, and my students Emily and Rebecca at The Ethical Culture Fieldston School.

Imaginary Gallery
A Collaborative Writing Exercise

by Stefania Heim

Conventional wisdom has it that the first example of ekphrasis — literature that engages a work of visual art — is the extended description of the shield Hephaistos forges for Akhilleus in Book 18 of Homer's *Iliad*. This famous passage consists of 150 lines (in Robert Fitzgerald's translation) of richly detailed "noble scenes": market places and weddings; besiegers, battles, and deaths; oxen plowing fields; a boy playing mournfully on a harp; two lions "rending the belly" of a bull; young girls dancing and holding each other by the waist. It is also conventional wisdom that no physical shield on earth could possibly hold everything Homer describes here. This first ekphrastic passage is utterly made up.

I find that ekphrastic writing assignments, in which students generate written work from an encounter with a visual object, can be very productive in the classroom. Ekphrasis forces writers to reckon concretely with the "image made of words" poetry teachers so often seem to be talking about: How can you get your own language to give rise, *in someone else's mind*, to what you see? Which aspects need describing? How much of the scene must you set? More, ekphrasis is a practice: a repeatable exercise in attention, an application, an act of translation between world and word.

The activities collected under the banner of ekphrasis, too, can help allay some of the anxiety of the search for a subject, of the blank page. And, there are so many ways for a poet to animate her encounter with a visual artifact. There is direct description; ventriloquism, by which I mean speaking as a figure in a work or as the artist; resistance to the art (a kind of hate poem or interrogation of the maker); meditation on the moment of viewing that projects outward to capture a larger swath of the viewer's experience (Rainer Maria Rilke's famous conclusion gazing upon the "Archaic Torso of Apollo," "You must change your life."). Ekphrasis is always an encounter. It is a way in.

Like Homer's shield, the assignment Imaginary Gallery is born at that magical point where seeing and imagining meet. Students will not actually *look* with their *eyes* at art; you do not need to take them to a museum. (Though, if you can, you should!) It is also a collaborative endeavor: in pairs, students take turns describing a work of art that has made an impression on them and composing poems from their partner's descriptions.

Imaginary Gallery might be built into a larger set of ekphrastic lessons. Or, it might be a stand-alone chance to get at some of the productive excitement of making something in response and in collaboration. No poem, of course, exists by itself alone. Art is always in conversation with the art that comes before, after, around, and beside it. And, our experience of art is never pure, but always mediated. This exercise takes such conversation and mediation as its joyful starting point.

Preparatory Writing/Brainstorming

The first step is to help students think of a work of art that interests them enough that they will be able to riff on it, and the experience of viewing it, for four minutes. If you haven't been talking with them regularly about art, they will likely need some priming. I start by telling them a story, or a couple of stories, about encounters I have had with visual works. I remember the first time I saw a video installation by Pipilotti Rist: the overwhelming feeling of being immersed under water, glimpses of a body swimming, bright aquamarine projected on two full walls, the artist occasionally screeching along to the maudlin music. I might also describe something more intimate: a quilt my grandmother made, or watching my father spray-paint a wooden sculpture in our backyard. With each story, I emphasize a different aspect of my encounter: with Rist, the sheer sensory experience; with my family's work, the feelings that come with remembering. I invite students to share their own preliminary glimmers, which I hope spark additional ideas for classmates. Once we've talked for a bit, I invite them to the page. They use free-writing as a tool for thinking and remembering, generating material, getting in the mood. I remind them that it's never too late to change course: it might take a whole page of writing about one encounter to arrive at a different one that truly clicks.

With more experienced students, or those who have been thinking in an inter-arts context in which this is just one in a series of exercises, I might jump right in with the interactive component of the lesson. Jumping in can be exciting because it gives students a chance to think out loud, discovering and creating the artwork in their minds as they try to describe it to their partner. Talking in a free-associative way, they won't have the chance to self-edit or decide in advance what might or might not be worth including. This can give their speech — and in turn, their classmate's poem — freshness and a quality of surprise.

Once students are ready, I divide them into pairs. They will have four minutes each to describe their art to their partner: what it looked like, where they saw it, how the experience made them feel, if they saw the piece again, its history, what they remember about the artist, the day they saw it, who they were with, what that person said, ate. Even with preparatory writing, four minutes is a long time to talk. Students simply won't be able to chart out in advance everything they are going to say. As a result, there will still be drifts, associations, and surprises. This kind of talking can be generative. Circulating around the classroom, I am attentive to lulls and I encourage students to free associate, to let the talking and imagining lead them, to remember with all their senses.

The listening partner does not interrupt. She listens silently while taking the most extensive notes she can manage. She tries to see the image her partner is painting while she is at the same time attentive to how her partner speaks: pauses, rushes, digressions, turns of phrase. Generally, the partners take turns talking and listening before anyone writes. This has the advantage of creating that shared, humming space of communal creation. The obvious disadvantage is that the person who listens first experiences a lapse of time between listening and writing. But, since the goal of these poems is never — could never be — "accuracy" or fidelity to the artwork, this might open up interesting possibilities or cross-pollination between descriptions.

Once everyone has spoken and listened in turn, we return to our places with our notes, the material of our poems. The instruction is, simply: *Write an ekphrastic poem describing this work you have never seen. You may use everything on your page, including direct quotations. Try to capture something of your partner's emotion in the encounter, something of their cadence in talking. What excited them, looking? What excited you, listening?* I might give students a length constraint: *Pare all of this down to just four lines.* After they've written these four-line versions, I might ask them to go home and write a second, twenty-line poem, drawing from the same or different elements of their encounter.

Imaginary Gallery is an exercise in remembering, noticing, listening, and imagining. How can we see sharply, feel acutely, through our own and another's eyes?

These poems were written by college students.

By the Batting of Your Lash

A giant's eye blinks, sticks there — cones of
color at full capacity. A glint of scale
hints at the begging ladies like drapery unfolds
the blind spot: man on the marble, making his hunger known.

Chloe Kaplan

Untitled

Four ballerinas — red, green, blue, you —
jumped out from a feeling book
that is a mirror inside-out
and can just help falling upside-down.

Gabriel Wexler

Not meant for you

The words are on all fours
pacing the room: scrawled prophesies,

  obscured dreaming,
the vascular and secret language of women.

before and after the overture
the women's backs are turned

and you'll make lines
out of the room's eight

  overlooked planes
or take her side in your fist

or first sidle up and say hey there
what's on your mind

and you'll notice
when thoughts are birds they don't

  even look beautiful
they just trail their own curious hands along

their own red satin waists.
in this room of faceless freedoms

the words call out to each other
  and the women's backs

are 9th and 10th iterations on how to dream
without giving it away.

Ivy Spiegel Ostrom

Beyond Imitation
Reverse Engineering the Lyric Poem

by Brian Blanchfield

In my sixteen years of teaching poetry — at levels from high school to graduate school — I have developed a practice of working with generative writing prompts and constraints. I have come to understand that part of training as a writer at any level is to (re)acquaint yourself with the resilience of English and your own resourcefulness, which are mutually productive as it turns out. The following are two prompts I have used to reliably good effect, two of the most generative. Each of these moves well beyond imitation exercises — indeed, in particular ways they necessitate discovery and autonomy — and they both have a way of bypassing inhibition. Part of my job as a teacher, as I see it, is to get developing writers out into the field of the poem, making decisions (learning experientially), before they determine that the task of writing poetry is impossible.

Then and Then Some

1. Share excerpts from the book-length (life-long) prose poem by Joe Brainard, *I Remember*. The book is built entirely of sentences and short paragraphs that begin "I remember." There are more than a thousand of these entries, each of which relates a discrete memory. Read the excerpts aloud and familiarize yourselves with the rhythm of his procedure.

    Whereas Brainard's project is to recollect moments across his lifetime — from his childhood in Tulsa to his life as an artist in New York — achronologically, this writing exercise means to drill down on and reveal primarily one moment.

2. Ask your students to draw a line that bisects a blank page vertically, so that two tall columns are created. As more than one page may be needed, they might draw the line on a second sheet or on the reverse as well.

3. Say to your students: *Select a moment from your own life. It needn't be the most significant moment of your life (but it may be), but it should be a moment — from last Sunday, or from eleven years ago — that you feel you can recall well, perhaps for reasons inexplicable to you.*

Make sure you have selected a single moment. A split-second. Not a whole afternoon, or an entire encounter, but one moment within it. Stick to this one moment; e.g., not the difficult conversation I had with my sister last year, but the moment in that conversation when she turned her head away... .

4.   In the left column, students should write I-remember sentences that capture what can be recollected about that moment. Encourage them to take recourse in all five senses, and interior sensations as well as exterior data. "I remember I saw the rain across town, at the foot of the mountains, but it was still dry on our sidewalk," or "I remember in my left jeans pocket my phone was vibrating, though it would be hours before I would see that Mark was worried about me."

5.   Meanwhile, in the right column, have them write I-remember sentences that capture any stray associations or memories *before or since* the chosen moment. (One needn't know why he or she is making these associations.) For example, "I remember my mother's hands were always cold," or "I remember practicing my new signature in the air with sparklers the summer I was adopted. It might have seemed I was conducting some private melody."

Encourage them to fill both columns. Permit writing for about twenty minutes.

6.   Then, when time has expired, there is a brief but important Phase Two: Ask them read over the page(s) and re-sequence their sentences, in whatever order makes intuitive sense to them, intermixing left and right columns, using numbering or arrows or whatever method is simplest.

7.   Ask volunteers to read aloud.

8.   Invite them then, at home, to type out the poem and, over the course of the next week, eliminate most or all instances of the phrase "I remember" (consider substituting other anaphora)

and revise the poem for qualities the student wants in it: music, associative logic, lineation, concision, connective syntax, poignancy, etc.

*

In a certain way, Then and Then Some is an exercise that reverse engineers the lyric poem; the draft that emerges is compulsively concerned with a single fraught moment, which — however clarifying the attention to particulars — attains mystique and which is not hastened into narrative advancement. Often students produce a poem that is personal, yes, but also a little self-mysterious.

It can be illuminating, during consideration of these poems, to read with students a few published autobiographical lyric poems and compare their attributes with those of the students' work, and imagine together how the poems might have been similarly drafted. Philip Larkin's "To the Sea," Louise Glück's "Vespers [You thought we didn't know]," Alan Shapiro's "Sleet," Carl Phillips' "Corral," and Catherine Barnett's "Memento Mori" are all poems that reward such study.

Here are passages from revised student poems, some of them notably quite inventive with step 8.

> Imagine rushing to the other room and shutting the door.
> Imagine saying "nobody" when your mother asks who it is.
> It is your sister, her daughter, talking about your mother. This is taking
> the call in the other room, imagine.
> Imagine having always felt a sort of paralysis answering phone calls.
> Hello, prompt.
> Imagine having never really made an effort to get to know your dad.
> It is your sister choking up. Prompt. Imagine something sufficient to say.
> Imagine your mother being, in the next room, the reason to close
> the door.
> Imagine the door, years before, closed, your father asleep in the
> living room.

*

When I remember fishing with my uncle, I remember the first and last time
I shot an animal. I was nine, it was a brown cottontail, and I cried.
When I remember being in the front seat of some girl's car, I remember
      she was
crying. Some girl, crying, why? When I remember
sleeping in parks, the tea gets cold, the fading away my life you might say.
      Remember,
it was raining. When I remember the fort in the hills where I drank with
my friends in middle school, I remember the dream I had the night before
my mother died. When I remember my number written on the dashboard,
I'm letting the tea get cold. I remember thinking I was dead. Having
no shoes on.

*

Sometimes, lying beneath trees, it's feeling the sunlight, not seeing it
through the branches you remember, though your eyes are open.
Sometimes it is cold when the sun is out.
Sometimes it takes the cold to see how satisfying, in the cold,
      a cigarette is.
Once I went to the park with my dad and spent the whole time crying
      because
he wouldn't push me harder on the swings.
Sometimes the smell of pine is how it sticks to your fingers.
Why wasn't he, like the other dads, just doing it?
Sometimes, when there are children around, you feel bad for smoking
with your friends on a hike. You see yourselves in one another's example.
Sometimes it takes the cold, when the sun is out, to determine
the pinecone, on the other hand, smells of nothing.

Self-Governance

This next prompt is for more advanced students, though it has a
more childish origin point. It starts with a cartoon many of us grew
up watching in syndication on Saturday mornings. Each episode of
The Road Runner was created according to precise parameters, in
a method that you might sooner imagine was a conceptual artist's.
The creator, Chuck Jones, wrote out and distributed to his cel

animators a list of nine esoteric rules that he insisted each episode of *The Road Runner* observe. Among the nine rules were:

- No dialogue ever, except "beep-beep!"
- The road runner must stay on the road — otherwise, logically, he would not be called road runner.
- All action must be confined to the natural environment of the two characters — the Southwest American desert.
- The coyote is always more humiliated than harmed by his failures.
- All materials, tools, weapons, or mechanical conveniences must be obtained from the Acme Corporation.
- Whenever possible, make gravity the coyote's greatest enemy.

If you and your students have seen any of the more than forty episodes of *The Road Runner*, you will recognize these defining characteristics. In a way, Jones, creating art with the use of constraints, was ensuring a kind of formal regularity and consistent artistic character of his cartoon.

Imagine for a moment that, watching an episode without knowing anything of Jones' method, you are able to derive the rules that seem to govern the composition. This thought experiment guides the prompt at hand. Except, instead of a six-minute cartoon, the object of study is a poem.

This is a good prompt to use with students when reading and studying potentially difficult poetry together. Let's say you've read Marianne Moore's "The Mind Is an Enchanting Thing," or James Schuyler's "Freely Espousing," or Eduardo Corral's "Acute Immune Deficiency Syndrome," or Robyn Schiff's "Gate," or Patrick Rosal's "Brooklyn Antediluvian." Challenging poems that reward study. You might have others. Have at hand the poem your students want to examine. And ask each of them to perform the following experiment:

1. Read and reread closely the poem you have selected as uniquely compelling or successful. It could be your favorite poem of the class, or one that beguiles you. Consider how it is made — line, stanza, structure, rhetoric, melody — and consider what aspects make the poem successful or memorable.

2. Imagine that this poem is, in fact, a type (in the same away that any single episode of *The Road Runner* might be typical of the whole series). Write out nine rules that seem to govern the realm and/or the composition of this poem.

3. List them, and give them the imperative syntax of rules. The more particular the better. Be sure to include rules that you genuinely think are responsible for some of the poem's success. For instance:

   - The poem must have at least four times as many lines as sentences.
   - It is only at the turning point of the poem that the abstraction in the title is repeated.
   - The speaker must address a "you" and must confide in the addressee straight away.
   - The poem will report the news of the day, but only as if incidentally.
   - No line of the poem may be longer than six beats; the longest rhymes with the one that follows.
   - The poem should contain two questions, one an elaboration of the other.

4. When you have written out nine rules you like for their aptness and concision, you have your completed list. Now put the poem out of sight, and do not refer to it again.

5. Here's the catch. *Your* next poem, the one you write for next week, must satisfy each of the rules in the list you have written. Do not attempt to imitate the original poem; rather, adhere to the rules you have articulated as if they were a new set of instructions or guidelines. In essence, they are.

The draft that emerges is, interestingly, not an imitation of the original poem. But it is, in a manner of speaking, a sibling of the original poem. The resourcefulness necessary to manage and satisfy all of the nine directives often produces an agile poem that is unique: characteristic of the student poet's work but with an uncanny new quality — sometimes a kind of aplomb or dispassionate poise. I have found that to be the case when I have used this exercise, mapping a Merrill Gilfillan poem I like, and writing from the rules I had derived for it. I even found that the procedure could be repeated; after my first such poem, I reset and wrote another, and another: a series of three poems that abided by the rules I'd written. And each of those poems were also siblings, sharing a curious resemblance that is not immediately noticeable. They are some of my favorite poems.

These two exercises are, I suppose, part of a greater pedagogical project: to thaw the inhibiting and self-defeating expectation that there is a one-to-one transfer of thought to expression; that first you decide on an idea for a poem, and then you execute the poem that delivers the idea. A good prompt or procedural sets up the propitious conditions for *discovery* to take place, and it is the sense of a writer discovering within a developing piece that makes the work obliging and revelatory to the reader. It is something I myself have to learn again and again as a writer, and it can only be learned by doing.

Undressing Advertisements

Poetry as Feminist Critique through Harryette Mullen's *Trimmings*

by Jennifer Firestone

I teach Harryette Mullen's *Trimmings* in a college-level course I've co-created with poet Marcella Durand: Feminist Avant-garde Poetics. Mullen describes her intent in *Trimmings* as the following: "…I wanted the book to be about feminist ideas, a feminist exploration of how femininity is constructed using clothing, how the clothing itself speaks to, or is emblematic of, certain kinds of constraints on women's bodies."

In this course, I take several preparatory steps before teaching *Trimmings* to ground the students and contextualize the work. First, I assign a selection of Gertrude Stein's *Tender Buttons*. *Trimmings* is not only in conversation with *Tender Buttons*, but it subversively critiques Stein's silence on race and other social constructions within language. I also assign Stein's essay "Poetry and Grammar," which provides further insight into Stein's complex theories of syntax and punctuation, allowing students to understand some of the language structure of *Tender Buttons* and, hence, the structure of *Trimmings*.

While I can recommend teaching the following lesson within this context, *Trimmings* can also be used as a discrete lesson that offers students the opportunity to question—and playfully subvert—social constructions of gender. You can begin by sharing a selection of Mullen's short prose pieces, such as the poem that opens the collection:

Trimmings
Hareyette Mullen

Becoming, for a song. A belt becomes such a small waist. Snakes around her, wrapping. Add waist to any figure, sub-tract, divide. Accessories multiply a look. Just the thing, a handy belt suggests embrace. Sucks her in. She buckles. Smiles, tighter. Quick to spot a bulge below the belt.

As students begin to read the poems in *Trimmings*, they come to understand that the "thinking" is operating and flexing on many levels. Language is active—no word sits alone without reverberations of its lineage or associations. Mullen's work is not a performance of language play for language play's sake. There is a deep cutting critique and commentary that invite all aspects of identity (e.g., gender, class, race, and sexuality) to be interrogated. In this way, Mullen's poetry reflects one of the quintessential impulses behind the Feminist Avant-garde.

Even from the get go, Mullen makes it clear that we will be examining language and ideas on a microscopic level. The title, *Trimmings*, itself conjures images of garnish around a festive dinner, or holiday, and also, given the topic of this book, accessories that a woman might wear. What might it mean to equate those two images — garnish on a platter of food and garnish on a woman's body? The adjective "trim" is tucked into *Trimmings*, which evokes our culture's obsession with women being slender, and also "trim" as a verb, suggesting the work of a seamstress or a plastic surgeon. Or trimmings as the "stuff" that gets left behind, marginalized and looked at as waste. The list of associations is endless.

This critique latent within her work does not forego the immense pleasure also to be found there. Read any of Mullen's lines out loud and you'll hear the beat, the tight rhythms, and the slipperiness of the words as they slosh together and nod to other associations:

The color "nude," a flesh tone. Whose flesh unfolds barely, appealing tan. Shelf life of stacked goods. Body stalking software inventories summer stock. Thin-skinned Godiva with a wig on horseback, body cast in a sit calm.

Each time one reads a poem from *Trimmings*, a new understanding of the hidden puns, innuendos, and aphorisms is revealed. Mullen's work is connected to music; the reader can catch threads of jazz and blues. The poems are alive and beckoning, but not without a pointed critique of what is actually being sung.

As a class we discuss the structure and form of Mullen's series: the use of lists, the prose poem, and the function of metonomy and parataxis. The following excerpt is especially helpful as a lead-in to the student writing:

Two shapely legs stretch, then run. Sheer magic, a box di-
vided. One saw a woman cut in half, waving incredible feet.

I like this poem because it is rich in allusions (magic meshed with the disembodied woman), along with what appears to be pantyhose advertising copy: "Sheer magic," "run." Once students have a clearer sense of how these poems operate, I assign what I call "the experiment." I choose the word "experiment" over "exercise" because I want to focus on the excitement of risk-taking—the unknowingness that can occur in poem-making. The experiment I give to my students is as follows:

Find a fashion advertisement that intrigues you, irritates you, enrages you, or captures your attention. This image should be accompanied by suggestive text that you can appropriate, recycle, or subvert. Once you have examined the advertisement closely, write a poem that responds to it. In writing this piece, try to subtly embed your critique of the advertisement into the poem, but not to the detriment of the imaginative and exciting writing that hopefully will evolve. Some poetic tools to experiment with include listing, parataxis, and lots of slippery word play and sonic possibility (such as punning and double entendre). Be as compressed and tight in your writing as possible, eliminating any excess language.

If you want to fit this lesson into a single class meeting, you can bring in ready-made images for the students to choose from. Once students have selected their ads, you also can incorporate a pre-writing exercise to get them started. I sometimes begin by asking students to list the associations and wordplay developed from the language and images within their ads. I encourage them to play with synonyms and homonyms in order to begin to develop associations.

The results are phenomenal. Students tend to select highly provocative ads to work with and then their imagination takes off. In the following poems, students unpack the advertisements of Bally accessories and a Windsmoor suit. Each poem's burst of sound and image reel from line to line, captivating a reader almost as quickly as the ads from which they were plucked.

hair, blown. wild and free, the mountain and we. legs, bare. probably by nair. gazelle. protected by thin straps criss cross. lean with it, rock with it. curve your curb, to curve your vessel. work with it. S. chest.

Tia Toney (College)

A 100% worsted flannel modesty. Very proper pick-and-pick the worst felt feeling. You know it keeps you tight. Dark neutral colors suit you. Means business. Pearls and flowers, you know it's good. Look your best label. Hold your umbrella in sleek leather gloves. Look your 100% best worsted suit size small.

Kallie Quist (College)

Shadow Poems
Creative Exercises
for Revision

by Rosamond S. King

Do you remember playing "telephone," when the last person's message is a laughable version of the original one? Or playing "shadows," when one person makes faces and creates shapes with their body that their partner has to mimic, but often doesn't do exactly the same way? This Shadow Poems exercise draws upon those childhood games to create an exercise that encourages both revision and new writing.

Students — and the rest of us — sometimes struggle with revision, with how to take poems that have some value but that are not quite *there* yet, and make them better. Shadow Poems ask the writer to consider the original work from different angles — and different colors and styles! It aims to get us to the core concepts and language that we should keep, while letting the rest go.

Instructions

Choose any poem you've written — one that you've struggled with revising or one that you really like tends to work best. For this exercise, you will write the "shadow" of that poem. The next day, you will write the shadow poem in slang. You will continue this process, working your way down the list of prompts at regular intervals — one a day, or maybe one a week, whichever pace makes sense.

1. Write the original poem's shadow.

2. Write the poem in slang.

3. Write the poem as an apology.

4. Write the poem saturated with yellow.

5. Write the poem dripping wet.

6. Write the poem without using the letter a.

7. Write the poem as an application form.

8. Write the poem in the style of a poet you really dislike.

9. Write the poem full of alliteration.

10. Write the above poem's shadow.

11. What other ways can you rewrite your original poem? The possibilities are endless!

As you can see below, the exercise involves variously paying attention to language, form, and content. This rewriting and revision exercise will clarify what core concepts, images, or language you are interested in right now. It will also help you generate new work — if a particular prompt leads you to write additional poems, that's great! As long as you create new writing, your "shadow poems" are a success.

This exercise works well towards the end of a course, giving students practice with revision, or can be introduced in the middle of the term for students to work on every week and occasionally compare, for instance, their "yellow" poems. In addition to creating out-of-the-ordinary lines for more interesting poems, this exercise has the added potential of generating a series of linked pieces.

The student examples below provide an idea of the directions this exercise can take. "In Offense of Vision" is followed by its revision as a contract titled "A Promissory Note." The second poem uses a completely different structure and tone from the original, but keeps the same themes. These examples show how writing "shadow poems" can lead to a series or chapbook of linked poems, or to less thematically and stylistically connected pieces.

In Offense of Vision

In the second grade
    Sugarhands started sliding her hands into my pants
    so I took a knife, & stabbed holes into my favorite belt.
    I don't know if I wanted to make it harder for her to invade me,

or if I just wanted to   play a part in my own trauma.

When the tightening of belts did nothing but bruise my waist,
     I learned another trick —
     I started pressing against my eyes with my forefingers
     so aggressively, it reshaped my corneas.
          In the normal eye they are perfectly curved
          hills. Mine look like teardrops that never got
          the chance to fall.

  I gave myself the difficult cure, a vision as focused
as a lie. What the doctors called astigmatism, I called coping.
It helped with everything:
                     Isiah is dead?
      Isiah is standing right in front of me,
      he doesn't even know what a bullet means.
                     Alex is dead?
      Alex is in the kitchen.
      She never got in the car.
      The car never crashed.

When Alex died,
     her name became the password
     to my old computer. I punched the keyboard
     as if I could type the pulse back into her.
          Don't look at me like a madman or a fool,
          all I did was the alter the way I saw
          my suffering. I pressed my sadness into
the easiest needle I could make of it
because I'd rather be a blind man
than an honest one.

For years I abused my eyes,
     the blooming colors like vertigo,
          It helped me mistake my parents'
     divorce for hand-holding.
     I needed to become dizzy towards it;
          I needed the car my father left in to look

like a boomerang so it could teach me
how to long for things promised to return.

My eyes are
      the hinges to this stupid door of a mouth;
      if a boy always saw the shadow of a man's hand
      flung across a kitchen,
      do not ask why

he reads the word,
touch like it's unpronounceable.

      I don't know if I turned my father into a weapon
      or if I was raised by weapon
      my eyes try to bend into a father.

I avoid his hands like Sugarhands, fearful of the strike,
            he'd probably choke my vision

      straight if he heard this.
I want to tell him that I learned from him,
         that most days my heart is the hardest thing to see.
That I open my eyes every morning,
hoping my guilt will scab into new skin.

Sean Des Vignes (Brooklyn College)

A Promissory Note

I'm stone. I'm flesh. — Yusef Komunyakaa

SOFT-PALM BANK

PROMISSORY NOTE

Principal	Loan Date	Maturity	Loan No.	Account	Officer	Initials
PALMS	3/2000	6/19/2013	00001	281991	God	

References in the tabled area are for Borrower's use only & do not limit the applicability of this document to any particular loan or item. Any item containing "God" should be disregarded due to faith limitations.

Borrower: Sean DesVignes	Lender: Sugarhands

PROMISE TO LEND: Sugarhands ("Lender") lends Sean DesVignes ("Borrower") palms. Unlawful money. This payment is to be received via Sugarhands' unbuckling of Sean's belt buckle/Sugarhands' right palm slow descent into Sean's underwear. The lender thrusts & rubs. Unless otherwise agreed, lender performs daily for a class period. The borrower is to receive all outstanding effects of this experience, [substitution of his heart for a stone, a leaving of rooms.] Lender. Perform. This act. Back of the classroom. The teacher cannot see. The lender acknowledges that this note is terminated if caught.

PROMISE TO BEND: Sean DesVignes ("Borrower") promises to lend Sugarhands ("Lender") sworn secrecy. Borrower. Ask for pleasure he cannot name. Borrower promises to never explore why it feels good, promises to know why it is wrong & continue to beg for it. Borrower helps lender pass all of her tests & quizzes in exchange for lending. This is his first transaction. Cuts a hole so far back into his belt that when he loops it there it bruises his waist as he walks. The lender does not lotion her hands.

POSTPAYMENT: Borrower agrees that all outstanding effects are deserved & earned fully. Borrower understands Lender only uses him because he's intelligent. Borrower promises to convince himself that the only reason he kept up in school was so Lender could open him. Borrower agrees not to fall in love with any woman & step backwards before any hug. Lender says "I just need your help." Borrower crafts a magic in which his zipper crawls down by itself, making Lender's job much easier.

Sean DesVignes (Brooklyn College)

The Poem as Divination Tool
The Tarot Card Exercise

by Dorothea Lasky

As a poet, I've always thought about poetry writing as a type of divination. I've been writing poems since I was seven, and in my early days, I used to write in the dark after being put to bed too early for my liking. Because I was writing into the literal darkness, I couldn't even see what I was writing down and instead felt for the words. I never knew early on that I was writing "poems" per se — I just knew that the voices came to me and urged me to write down their words. There was a sense of absolute freedom, as what I was writing wouldn't need to be corrected by a teacher for its misspellings or grammatical inconsistencies. I had an idea even then that the arbitrary rules of power through language do not matter to the dead. Although it would take many years before I read work by poets who felt the same way I did, I knew in my tiny beginning brain that something from the "Outside" — as Jack Spicer said, "as far away as those galaxies which seem to be sending radio messages to us" — were speaking to me, too.

In many ways, conjuring poems is still my process. I don't necessarily write at night, like I did as a little girl, and the ability to siphon off language from the air happens in strange and oftentimes unpredictable intervals during the day. Instead of having a plan for writing poems, my one singular eye of the spirits hopes to be open constantly to the loud or soft sounds, so that the voices who have given me the gift of poetry can speak to me whenever they need or wish to. For me, the cycle of what is behind language has been a ferocious state of constant salvation.

As a poetry teacher — at one point more to younger students and now mostly with adults — I feel my job is to teach all poets that the voices that long to speak through them are accessible as outside forces, and to write poems all they must do is ask them questions. One thing I hear over and over again from poets and writers is that they are blocked and can't think of the right language to say what they want, or worse yet, they can't think of any language at all. The trick, I think, to combat this feeling of unproductivity (or writer's block, as it's called) is to ask the atmosphere for what it wants to say.

Related to all of these ideas, a favorite exercise I love to do with my students is one where I ask them to think about poetry as a divination tool. It cements the important idea that poetry can and should be part of our everyday lives, and also can provide guidance and solace when we need answers to important questions. Before doing the exercise, we discuss the idea of poetry as a source of divination. I ask my students if they have practice using divination tools, like tarot cards, or if they have ever had a hard question and asked a poetry book for the answer.

For example, they might have done the latter — as I have done many times myself — by choosing a particular page or line at random from a poetry book and then by using their interpretative and analytic skills to decipher what the poem is "telling them." We discuss writers like WB Yeats, Nathaniel Mackey, Hannah Weiner, Sor Juana de la Cruz, Bhanu Kapil, Alice Notley, and, of course, Jack Spicer, who all have written in various ways about the idea of poetry writing as a kind of conjuring. We discuss how best to use this idea in positive ways in our future processes and practices, and then we do the exercise below.

Inspirational Texts

Once you start looking for it, you start to see that poems always have found ways to incorporate divinatory tools or texts, particularly the tarot deck. A favorite poem of mine by Sylvia Plath, "The Hanging Man," is a perfect example of how the imagery of a particular tarot card, in this case, The Hanged Man card, can inspire a poet to write a sort of ekphrastic poem about it.

The Hanging Man
Sylvia Plath

The Hanging Man

By the roots of my hair some god got hold of me.
I sizzled in his blue volts like a desert prophet.

The nights snapped out of sight like a lizard's eyelid:
A world of bald white days in a shadeless socket.

A vulturous boredom pinned me in this tree.
If he were I, he would do what I did.

Readers familiar with tarot likely see the man who is hanging in the tree on the card. The card itself is about sacrifice, and maybe Plath's poem is *about* the idea of sacrificing one's self to art or to have a divine calling. The Hanged Man card is also about feeling in a rut and needing to get out of it. Plath twists the poem so that we start to see her own persona hanging by legs in the card, stuck to the tree, even though in her poem "some god got hold of" the speaker "[b]y the roots of my hair." I've always felt that the person's expression in the actual card seemed peaceful, and so I love how Plath interprets the mood of her persona hanging from the tree as a "vulturous boredom." I often bring in this poem to use as a supplementary text to The Tarot Card Exercise, because it inspires divinatory writing, because it uses the tool of a tarot card as a place to write a poem from.

Another poem that deeply inspires the work I have students do in The Tarot Card Exercise is Bhanu Kapil's "What are the consequences of silence?" In this poem, the speaker is directly addressing a painting by Georgia O'Keefe titled "Red Canna."

**What are the
consequences
of silence?**
Bhanu Kapil

What are the consequences of silence?

53.

Red Canna, I see you. Edge of. What I saw: a flower blossoming,
in slow motion.
Not specific enough. Okay. *No.* Cannot. Red Canna, I veer into
you. I am not in
one straight line. Red Canna, I see you. 1904. The University of
Arizona Museum
of Art. Opening in slow motion: are you okay? Are you okay? Can
you hear me?
(*I can't*)

That's how it begins: impenetrable.

The book of two words I happen to see, out of the corner of my
eye, on a wall. Such
slowness.

These words took years to arrive.

Although this poem is not about the tarot specifically, it still speaks to the theme of the exercise very well. In the poem, Kapil's persona is presumably doing some ekphrastic work, albeit, at least in part, of a spiritual nature. What I've always loved about the poem and why it relates to The Tarot Card Exercise is that it's about how poets can communicate through layers of time and space via art. The poem seems to talk to O'Keefe's painting, asking it, "Are you okay?" and then eventually seeing words on the wall as its answer to that question, which read, "Such / slowness."

But then there is another layer of communication present in the exchange, as you can't completely tell if the persona is talking to the painting, or to the subject of the painting: the Red Canna flower. In the poem, O'Keefe's painting becomes "the tarot card" and her poem becomes the way to find out the answer to a question, which, the title states, is, "What are the consequences of silence?" The poem seems to answer that the consequence is probably the slowness of communication through layers of being: flower, painter, painting, poet, and poem (among other unseen things, too). Kapil's poem has inspired my own exercise below, especially as it raises a question in the title and then explores answers within the stanzas that follow.

These are only two examples of poems that serve as inspiration for the exercise and that work well to spark discussions about it. There are many others that could be fruitful jumping-off points and I hope when you do The Tarot Card Exercise with your students you find them!

The Tarot Card Exercise

I ask my students to bring the following materials to class:

- Three pieces of paper or cloth that each represent something from your past, present, and future respectively. (Also, make sure these are things you don't mind cutting up.)

- A burning question that you would like answered.

- Pens, markers, colored pencils, or anything else that you like to draw with.

- A piece of paper or notebook to write in.

- I supply the tarot deck (I usually use the Rider Waite deck, but you can use any deck you like) and blank notecards (I usually use 3x5 inches, but any size can work). Once students are situated at their tables or desks, I distribute three blank notecards to each person. Then I give the following instructions, circulating supplies as necessary throughout the process. The times indicated are for each student, and obviously you will need to take into account how long it might take for each student to select three cards from the tarot deck if you have a large class:

1. Select a Past, Present, and Future card from the tarot deck. (1 minute)

2. "Translate" what you see on each tarot card onto your three notecards. You can interpret however you wish, but the idea is that you might not draw exactly what you see. That is to say, if the leaves of a tree stand out to you, feel free to draw a whole card full of leaves. (20-30 minutes)

3. Affix the cloth and paper you have brought in to the corresponding cards; i.e. put your cloth/paper from your past on your Past card, your cloth/paper from your present on your Present card, and your future cloth/paper on your Future card. (5-10 minutes)

4. Once you have created three original cards, you are now going to use them to write a poem. It will be four stanzas long. The first three stanzas can be any length you wish, but the fourth stanza will only be one line.

5. Look at your first card, which is your Past card. This card represents all of the energy you have carried with you to the

situation you are asking about. Describe all the things you bring to it. Include visual details from your card and ideas that arise spontaneously from your imagination in your first stanza. (10 minutes)

6. Now, look at your Present card. This card represents what the energy is swirling around the situation currently. Describe what is present in your second stanza. Include visual details from your card and ideas that arise spontaneously from your imagination in your second stanza and try to double the amount you had in your first stanza. (10 minutes)

7. Finally, look at your Future card. This card represents how this situation will be in your life in six to twelve months. Describe what this future situation will be in your third stanza. Include visual details from your card and ideas that arise spontaneously from your imagination in your third stanza and try to double the amount you had in your second stanza. (10 minutes)

8. For your last line, begin with the phrase, "The answer is_____." Now fill in the blank. (5 minutes)

9. Title your poem with your burning question. (2 minutes)

10. Share your poem with everyone. Discuss what the poem is trying to tell you. Are you happy with the answer to your question — seen through the lens of the poem? Did the answer surprise you? What poem would you write next about your question and its answer?

I have done this exercise in numerous formal and informal class-rooms over the past few years and I've always seen it work well with my students. Students will express that they are surprised by the answer that they receive and how fun it is to make their new, translated tarot cards and new poems. Oftentimes students will edit the poems they write from the exercise into something new for workshop sessions, but the resonances of their original questions always seem to manage to shine through their poems in exciting ways. Below is one recent example to give you a feeling of the sorts of possibilities this exercise can inspire students to create.

Emily Skillings is a poet and a teacher. Her first book of poems, *Fort Not*, was published by The Song Cave in 2017. The cards she drew from the deck were the Knight of Cups, the Queen of Cups, and the King of Cups. Here are her translations of these cards:

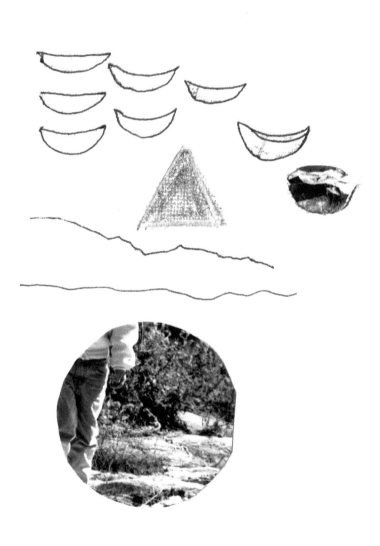

Here is her poem:

Are You Quite Sure What Will Happen to Me?

When I took my feet into their white shoes
and stepped out onto the rocks
how would I know what would be?
A fleet of moons falling
into the sea's crevices
A falling closer to hovering
than will ever come again
I have been told I lie or tend to exaggerate
The shorelines never did meet
I picked this up from a mouth
pink pouch of Wednesday
July 18, 1995

Is star anise a pod or a bulb
There is so much acid in me always
knocking about. Milk kills it. Sleep
prepares it. Each moment a present
dislodging from a dominant follicle
I drink the cloudy green pastis
from a small green Italian martini glass
plucked from a set of six
nesting on a mirrored tray
The observation I approach
as I add the water
is that my indifference to almost everything
is often mistranslated as worry
which sweeps it under
a burnt orange woven rug
It is pleasantly frayed along the edge

Considering a bowl
I took everything out
The therapist said it was gold

and I could slowly begin to add things back in
"What goes in your golden bowl?"
(This is another way of asking
what is important to me)
I think obviously of Henry James
the wrong kind of thing
what I'll never have. All is vanity.
My eyes are closed
but the bowl is blue
It will always be
What goes in my blue bowl
If I'm being perfectly honest
keep everything out
of it
but give it a lid. A closed world,
like an oyster. It may not be possible
to completely reinvent yourself
over the course of a few days
The line carries
a blurred arrow

The answer is a pearl lodged in a corner.

Emily Skillings

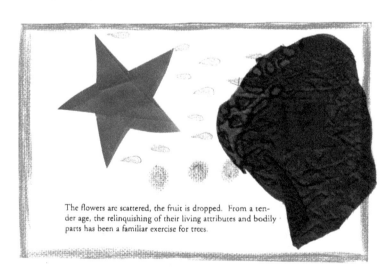

The flowers are scattered, the fruit is dropped. From a tender age, the relinquishing of their living attributes and bodily
parts has been a familiar exercise for trees.

It is a world categorically closed in upon itself.

Contributors

Brain Blanchfield is the author of three books of prose and poetry, most recently *Proxies: Essays Near Knowing*, for which he received a 2016 Whiting Award in Nonfiction; and *A Several World*, which won the 2014 Academy of American Poets' James Laughlin Prize. He lives in Moscow, Idaho, where he teaches in the MFA program at the University of Idaho.

Matthew Burgess is an assistant professor at Brooklyn College. He is the author of a poetry collection, *Slippers for Elsewhere*, as well as several children's books, including *Enormous Smallness: A Story of E. E. Cummings*. After completing his doctorate at the CUNY Graduate Center, Matthew edited an anthology of writing and visual art titled *Dream Closet: Meditations on Childhood Space*. He joined the Teachers & Writers Collaborative roster back in 2001 and continues to lead poetry workshops with early elementary students in New York City. Matthew also serves on the editorial board of *Teachers & Writers Magazine*.

Chris Cander is the award-winning author of the novels *The Weight of a Piano*, *Whisper Hollow*, and *11 Stories*; and the children's picture book *The Word Burglar*. For seven years, she has been a writer-in-residence for Writers in the Schools, serves on the literary nonprofit Inprint's advisory board, and stewards several Little Free Libraries in her community. A former competitive bodybuilder, Chris currently hold a 3rd dan in taekwondo and is a certified women's defensive tactics instructor. She lives in Houston with her husband and two children.

Tina Cane was born in Hell's Kitchen, NYC. She attended the University of Vermont, the Sorbonne, and completed her masters degree in French literature at the University of Paris IX-Nanterre. She is founder and director of Writers-in-the-Schools, RI, for which she works as a visiting poet. Tina is also an instructor with the writing community Frequency Providence. Tina's poems and translations have appeared in numerous journals, including *Spinning Jenny*, *Tupelo Quarterly*, *Cargo*, and *Two Serious Ladies*. Her work *The Fifth Thought* was published in 2008 and her collection *Once More with Feeling* appeared in 2017. Tina was the 2016 recipient of the Fellowship Merit Award in Poetry from the Rhode Island State Council on the Arts.

Todd Colby is a Brooklyn-based artist and poet focused on using words, images, and sounds to create poems, collages, paintings, and street art. He is the author of six books of poetry. Todd's most recent book, *Splash State*, was published by The Song Cave in 2014. His recent readings and exhibitions include MoMA PS1 Greater New York (2015), Dia Art Foundation (2015), Picture Room (2015), and Bureau Gassser (2017). Todd was on the faculty for the Ashbery Home School in 2016. He has been awarded The Fund for Poetry Award on two occasions. Todd received his BA in English literature from the University of Iowa.

Alex Cuff teaches classes in reading, writing, and restorative justice at the Academy for Young Writers, a 6–12 public school in East New York, Brooklyn. She advises Raven Press, a student-run small press that publishes student anthologies and chapbooks. Alex is co-founding editor of *No, Dear* magazine, a 2016 Poets House fellow, and a Pushcart Prize nominee. Her poetry and prose can be found online at *The Recluse*, *Apogee Journal*, and *Teachers & Writers Magazine*; and her chapbook, *Family, A Natural Wonder*, was published by Reality Beach in 2017.

Sarah Dohrmann has been a writer-in-residence with Teachers & Writers Collaborative since 2001. She also served as T&W's education director from 2011 to 2013. Sarah primarily writes creative nonfiction, which has appeared in various publications, including *Harper's Magazine*, *Tin House Magazine*, and *The Iowa Review*, among others. She also teaches writing for the Writing Institute, in Special Programs at Sarah Lawrence College, and in the Liberal Studies Program at New York University.

Melissa Febos is the author of the memoir *Whip Smart* (St. Martin's Press, 2010) and the essay collection *Abandon Me* (Bloomsbury, 2017). She is an associate professor of creative writing at Monmouth University.

Jennifer Firestone is the author of *Story* (Ugly Duckling Presse, forthcoming), *Ten* (BlazeVOX [books]), *Gates & Fields* (Belladonna* Collaborative), *Swimming Pool* (DoubleCross Press), *Flashes and Holiday* (Shearsman Books), Waves (Portable Press at Yo-Yo Labs), *from Flashes* and *snapshot* (Sona Books), and *Fanimaly* (Dusie Kollektiv). She co-edited, with Dina Teen Lomax, *Letters to Poets: Conversations about Poetics, Politics and Community* (Saturnalia Books) and is collaborating with Marcella Durand on *Other Influences*, a book about feminist avant-garde poetics. Jennifer is an assistant professor of literary studies at The New School's Eugene Lang College and is also director of the Academic Fellows pedagogy program.

Joanna Fuhrman is the author of five books of poetry, most recently *The Year of Yellow Butterflies* (Hanging Loose Press, 2015) and *Pageant* (Alice James Books, 2009). From 2002 to 2017, she worked as a teaching artist through Teachers & Writers Collaborative. She currently teaches poetry and multimedia writing at Rutgers University and coordinates the Introduction to Creative Writing classes. www.joannafuhrman.com

Aracelis Girmay is the author of the poetry collections *Teeth*, *Kingdom Animalia*, and *the black maria*. As an educator, she has facilitated poetry workshops with people of all ages, from people in pre-school to adults. Aracelis is from Southern California and lives with her family in New York.

Stefania Heim is author of the poetry collections *HOUR BOOK*, chosen by Jennifer Moxley as winner of the Sawtooth Prize and forthcoming in 2019 with Ahsahta Books; and *A Table That Goes on for Miles* (Switchback Books, 2014). She is the recipient of a 2019 Translation Fellowship from the National Endowment for the Arts. *Geometry of Shadows*, her book of translations of metaphysical artist Giorgio de Chirico's Italian poems, will be published in 2019 by APS Books. Stefania has taught in colleges all around the US; pre-K in Genoa, Italy; and as a visiting poet in New York and Chicago public schools.

Amina Henry is a Brooklyn-based playwright, essayist, and teaching artist. As a playwright her work has been produced and/or developed by, among others, Clubbed Thumb, Ars Nova, Page 73, National Black Theatre, Oregon Shakespeare Festival, Project Y Theatre, Interrobang Theatre, The New Group, New Light Theater Project, The Flea, SUNY Purchase, and Brooklyn College. As a teaching artist, she has worked with Teachers & Writers Collaborative, Hunts Point Alliance for Children, Superhero Clubhouse, and the Shakespeare Society. She was a resident teaching artist at the Oregon Shakespeare Festival from 2009 to 2011. Amina is currently an adjunct lecturer at Brooklyn College.

Susan Karwoska is a writer, editor, and teacher. She is the recipient of a New York Foundation for the Arts (NYFA) Fellowship in Fiction, a Lower Manhattan Cultural Council Workspace residency for emerging artists, and residencies at Ucross and at Cummington Community of the Arts. From 2005 to 2014, she was the editor of *Teachers & Writers Magazine*, and she currently serves on its editorial board. Susan is also on NYFA's artist advisory board and the board of the NY Writers Coalition. She has written and edited for a variety of publications; lives in Brooklyn, New York; and is at work on a novel.

Rosamond S. King is a creative and critical writer and performer. Poetry publications include the Lambda Award-winning collection *Rock | Salt | Stone* and poems in more than three dozen journals, blogs, and anthologies. She has taught creative workshops at colleges, universities, literary festivals, and museums. Her scholarly book, *Island Bodies: Transgressive Sexualities in the Caribbean Imagination*, received the Caribbean Studies Association best book award. Rosamond is the creative editor of sx salon: a small axe literary platform and associate professor at Brooklyn College, part of the City University of New York. www.rosamondking.com

Jason Koo is the author of three full-length collections of poetry: *More Than Mere Light*, *America's Favorite Poem*, and *Man on Extremely Small Island*. He is also the author of the chapbook *Sunset Park* and co-editor of the *Brooklyn Poets Anthology*. An associate teaching professor of English at Quinnipiac University, Jason is the founder and executive director of Brooklyn Poets and creator of the Bridge (poetsbridge.org). He lives in Brooklyn.

Dorothea Lasky is the author of five books of poetry, most recently *Milk* (Wave Books, 2018). She is an associate professor of poetry at Columbia University's School of the Arts.

Caron Levis (MFA, LMSW) is — after many reVISIONS — the author of several picture books, including *Stop That Yawn!* (Atheneum), *May I Have A Word?* (FSG), and the award-winning *Ida, Always* (Atheneum), which the *New York Times* called, "an example of children's books at their best." A proud former Teachers & Writers Collaborative facilitator, Caron currently teaches and advises in The New School's Writing for Children/YA MFA program, works as a grief counselor, and loves using drama and writing to explore social, emotional, and literacy skills with kids of all ages through her author workshops. Visit her at www.caronlevis.com.

Erika Luckert is a writer from Edmonton, Canada, and a winner of the 92Y/*Boston Review* Discovery Prize. Her work has appeared in *Denver Quarterly*,

Indiana Review, CALYX, Room Magazine, Tampa Review, F(r)iction, Atticus Review, Boston Review, and others. Erika holds an MFA in poetry from Columbia University and lives in New York City, where she teaches creative and critical writing. www.erikaluckert.com

Sheila Maldonado is a lifelong writer and native New Yorker. She has taught student writers at virtually every grade level in NYC public schools. She currently teaches writing for the City University of New York. Sheila is the author of the poetry collection *one-bedroom solo* (Fly by Night Press, 2011) and the forthcoming collection *that's what you get* (Brooklyn Art Press). She is a CantoMundo Fellow and a Creative Capital awardee as part of desveladas, a visual writing collective.

Peter Markus is the senior writer at InsideOut Literary Arts in Detroit. His most recent book is *Inside My Pencil: Teaching Poetry in Detroit Public Schools.*

Jasminne Mendez is a poet, educator, and award-winning author. She has had poetry and essays published by or forthcoming in *The Acentos Review, Crab Creek Review, Kenyon Review, Gulf Coast, The Rumpus,* and others. She is a senior contributing editor at Queen Mob's Teahouse and the author of two poetry/prose collections, *Island of Dreams* (Floricanto Press, 2013), which won an International Latino Book Award; and *Night-Blooming Jasmin(n)e: Personal Essays and Poetry* (Arte Publico Press, 2018). Jasminne is a 2017 CantoMundo Fellow and an MFA candidate in the creative writing program at the Rainier Writer's Workshop at Pacific Lutheran University.

Emily Moore teaches English, particularly the Poetry Workshop classes, at Stuyvesant High School in New York City. Her chapbook, *Shuffle,* is available through Paper Nautilus Press. She may or may not be the only person to have read a sonnet about Beyoncé on NPR.

Michael Morse teaches at The Ethical Culture Fieldston School and the Iowa Summer Writing Festival. His book of poems, *Void and Compensation,* was published by Canarium Books in 2015 and was a finalist for the 2016 Kate Tufts Discovery Prize.

Cait Weiss Orcutt's work has appeared in *Boston Review, Chatauqua, FIELD,* and others. Her poems have been nominated for a Pushcart Prize and Best New

Poets 2016, and her manuscript *VALLEYSPEAK* (Zone 3, 2017) won Zone 3 Press' 2016 First Book Award, judged by Douglas Kearney. Cait has an MFA from The Ohio State and is pursuing her PhD in poetry from the University of Houston. She consults on manuscripts with Tell Tell Poetry and teaches creative writing at the University of Houston, Grackle and Grackle, the Houston Flood Museum, the Jewish Community Center, Inprint, the Menil Collection, the Salvation Army, and Writers in the Schools. Cait lives in Houston with her husband Jimmy and her two rescue cats, Nib and Truckboat.

Bianca Stone is a poet and visual artist. Her books include *Someone Else's Wedding Vows* (Tin House, 2014), *Poetry Comics from the Book of Hours* (Pleiades, 2016), and *The Mobius Strip Club of Grief* (Tin House, 2018). Her poems, poetry comics, and nonfiction have appeared in a variety of magazines, including *Poetry*, *jubilat*, *The New Yorker*, and *Georgia Review*. Bianca lives in Vermont.

Tiphanie Yanique has taught writing and literature at the pre-school, elementary, high school, and college levels and beyond. She is currently professor at Wesleyan University, where she directs the Creative Writing Program. Tiphanie is the author of the poetry collection *Wife*, which won the 2016 Bocas Prize in Caribbean poetry and the United Kingdom's 2016 Forward/ Felix Dennis Prize for a First Collection; and the novel *Land of Love and Drowning*, which won the 2014 Flaherty-Dunnan First Novel Award from the Center for Fiction, the Phillis Wheatley Award for Pan-African Literature, and the American Academy of Arts and Letters Rosenthal Family Foundation Award, and was listed by NPR as one of the Best Books of 2014. Her collection of stories, *How to Escape from a Leper Colony*, won her a listing as one of the National Book Foundation's 5Under35. Tiphanie is from the Virgin Islands.

Permissions

Keith Althaus, "Little Elegy" from *Ladder of Hours: Poems 1969–2005*. Copyright © 2005 by Keith Althaus. Reprinted with the permission of The Permissions Company, Inc., on behalf of Copper Canyon Press, www.coppercanyonpress.org.

"The Black Lace Fan My Mother Gave Me," from *Outside History: Selected Poems 1980–1990* by Eavan Boland. Copyright © 1990 by Eavan Boland. Used by permission of WW Norton & Company, Inc.

Gwendolyn Brooks, "The Bean Eaters" and "Infirm." Reprinted by consent of Brooks Permissions.

"Track 4: Reflections as performed by Diana Ross" and "Track 5: Summertime as performed by Janis Joplin" from *Please*. Copyright 2008 by Jericho Brown. Reprinted by permission of New Issues Poetry & Prose.

"a poem is a city" from *The Days Run Away Like Wild Horses Over the Hills* by Charles Bukowski. Copyright © 1969 by Charles Bukowski. Reprinted by permission of HarperCollins Publishers.

Matthew Burgess, "Dear David." Used with permission of the author.

Chen Chen, "Self-Portrait With & Without." Used with permission of the author.

"Childhood's Retreat" by Robert Duncan, from *Ground Work: Before the War*, copyright © 1984 by Robert Duncan. Reprinted by permission of New Directions Publishing Corp.

t'ai freedom ford, "big bang theory." Used with permission of the author.

"On the First Day She Made Birds." From *When Living Was a Labor Camp* by Diana García. © 2000 The Arizona Board of Regents. Reprinted by permission of the University of Arizona Press.

Ross Gay, "The Truth" from *Against Which*. Copyright © 2006 by Ross Gay.

Index of Poems, Poets, and Poetic Form

Alexander, Elizabeth, 9

Alexie, Sherman, 9

Althaus, Keith, "Little Elegy," 180

Anaphora, xiii, 5, 200

Auden, WH, 9

Bird, Hera Lindsay, 10

Blues poem, 106–116

Boland, Eavan, "The Black Lace Fan My Mother Gave Me," 185

Brainard, Joe, 162, 198

Brock-Broido, Lucie, 2, 9

Brooks, Gwendolyn, "The Bean Eaters," 21

Brooks, Gwendolyn, "Infirm," 78

Brooks, Gwendolyn, "Queen of the Blues" (excerpt), 111

Brown, Jericho, "Track 4: Reflection as performed by Diana Ross," 13

Brown, Jericho, "Track 5: Summertime as performed by Janis Joplin," 14

Bukowski, Charles, "a poem is a city," 4, 9

Burgess, Matthew, "Dear David," 155

Carson, Anne, 9

Celan, Paul, 9

Char, René, 9

Chen, Chen, "Self-Portrait With & Without," 40

Cohen, Leonard, 10

Cole, Henri, 8

Coleridge, Samuel Taylor, 9

Doty, Mark, 179

Duncan, Robert, "Childhood's Retreat," 91

Ekphrasis, 76–81, 192

Elegy, 178–190

Enjambment, 23, 79, 94

Ferlinghetti, Lawrence, 10

ford, t'ai freedom, "big bang theory," 147

Free verse, 127, 130

Frost, Robert, 10

García, Diana, "On the First Day She Made Birds," 100

Gay, Ross, "The Truth," 119

Ginsberg, Allen, 23, 92, 153

Haiku, 19

Hayes, Terrance, "Carp Poem," 132

Hirsch, Edward, "Fast Break in Memory of Dennis Turner, 1946-1984," 128

Horace, 10

Howe, Marie, "What the Living Do," 181

Hughes, Langston, 110

Imitation, 36, 197-204

Johnson, Fenton, "Tired," 111

Kapil, Bhanu, "What are the consequences of silence?" 220

Kelly, Donika, "Love Poem: Mermaid," 173

Kelly, Donika, "Self-Portrait as a Door," 174

Kistulentz, Steve, 162

Koch, Kenneth, 9

Komunyakaa, Yusef, "Anodyne," 30

Larkin, Philip, 9

Lead Belly, "Good Morning Blues," 108

Lewis, J. Patrick, 10

Lorde, Audre, "Hanging Fire," 84

Lune, 18-28

MacLeod, Wendy, 10

Metaphor, 3, 33, 34, 38, 44-56, 59, 77, 100, 137, 149, 173, 182, 184

Metonomy, 207

Moore, Marianne, 137

Mullen, Harryette, Excerpts from *Trimmings*, 206-208

Myers, Walter Dean, *Blues Journey*, 112

Neruda, Pablo, 10

O'Hara, Frank, "Today," 154

Oliver, Mary, "Some Questions You Might Ask," 50

One-sentence poem, 127-135

Parataxis, 207-208

Park, Ishle Yi, "Ishle Yi Park is..." 39

Persona poem, 76-81

Plath, Sylvia, "The Hanging Man," 219

Pound, Ezra, 9

Repetition, 76-81, 82-88, 109, 112, 120, 149

Revision, 17, 34, 64-73, 92, 157, 210-216

Rilke, Rainer Maria, 46, 193

Rodríguez, Reina María, "first time," 121

Roux, Joseph, 10

Saadi, Yusuf, 10

Sandburg, Carl, 3, 10

Schulman, Grace, "Apples," 182

Shirali, Raena, "i know i am in love again when," 139

Simic, Charles, "Classic Ballroom Dances," 186

Smith, Danez, "dear white america," 145

Spicer, Jack, 218, 219

Stanford, Frank, "The Moon," 47

Stevens, Wallace, 162

Stone, Bianca, "Practicing Vigilance," 138

Stone, Ruth, "For a Post Card of My Mother at the Beach," 163

Synesthsia, 76

Tate, James, 10

Williams, William Carlos, "The Red Wheelbarrow," 20

Williams, William Carlos, "This is Just to Say," 153

Williams, William Carlos, "To a Poor Old Woman," 77

Zagajewski, Adam, "Self-Portrait," 36